THE vegan SCOOP

Text © 2009 Fair Winds Press

First published in the USA in 2009 by
Fair Winds Press, a member of
Quayside Publishing Group
100 Cummings Center
Suite 406-L
Beverly, MA 01915-6101
www.fairwindspress.com

13 12   4 5

ISBN-10: 1-59233-392-3

ISBN-13: 978-1-59233-392-9

Library of Congress Cataloging-in-Publication Data
Torro, Wheeler del.
   The vegan scoop : 150 recipes for dairy-free ice cream that
tastes better than the "real" thing / Wheeler del Torro.
      p. cm.
   Includes index.
   ISBN-13: 978-1-59233-392-9
   ISBN-10: 1-59233-392-3
   1. Non-dairy frozen desserts. I. Title.
TX795.T67 2010
641.8'13–dc22
                                    2008055936

Cover and book design: Kathie Alexander
Layout: Rachel Fitzgibbon, studio rkf
Photography: Jack Richmond Photography
   (except images on pages 4, 12, 34, 60, 82, 104, 126, 142, 174, 198,
   and 208 by Glenn Scott Photography, and images on pages 22,
   bottom 23, 24, 25, 26, 28, 30, and inset images on pages 43, 52,
   64, 71, 74, 85, 95, 99, 110, 123, 133, 134, 149, 153, 202, and 207
   by Eric Michael Photography)

Printed and bound in China

THE vegan SCOOP

150 Recipes for DAIRY-FREE ICE CREAM
That Tastes Better Than the "Real" Thing

WHEELER DEL TORRO

Founder and Owner of
Wheeler's Frozen Dessert Company

FAIR WINDS
PRESS
BEVERLY, MASSACHUSETTS

Contents

Preface 6

Introduction 13

Vegan Ice Cream: Best in Taste and Nutrition 14

Getting to Know Your Ingredients 16

Meeting Your (Ice Cream) Maker 31

Chapter 1   Classic Flavors 35

Chapter 2   Fruity Flavors 61

Chapter 3   Healthy Flavors 83

Chapter 4   Asian Flavors 105

Chapter 5   Caribbean and Island Flavors 127

Chapter 6   Novelty Flavors 143

Chapter 7   Aphrodisiacal Flavors 175

Chapter 8   Ice Cream Vessels and Sauces 199

Chapter 9   Ice Cream Sides and Desserts 209

Acknowledgments 234

About the "Inside Scoop" 235

Index 236

* A complete list of the recipes featured in
  this book can be found on page 239.

Preface

MY ICE CREAM DREAMS began at seventeen. Fresh out of high school and without a plan, I was in desperate need of "something to do" for the summer. At the time, I was dating a Parisian model named Max. She lived in New York City, but was moving back to France. She invited me to come with her and hang out for the summer. "Why not?," I thought. I could stay until August and then head off to college. Perfect.

For the first month, Max and I lived with her family in the south of France. Max's grandmother Estee did most of the cooking. She was an amazing cook. The trouble was, however, that Estee made a hobby out of scrutinizing my every move. She would watch me out of the corner of her eye, arms crossed, a scowl on her face. Despite her behavior (or maybe because of it), I started hanging out more in the kitchen, asking to set the table, stir a pot, chop an onion. Eventually, this little old woman relented and started showing me the secrets behind some of the most amazing foods I had ever tasted. For the rest of the summer, I learned how to make delicious soups, main courses, and desserts.

After a month living in the south, Max and I moved to Paris, where I spent my days seeing movies and plays, visiting museums, exploring, and above all else, visiting Berthillon, one of the great ice cream shops in the city. Sometimes I would wait for hours just to get a single-scoop cone. I could only imagine how much money the shop made.

Max would come with me when she wasn't working, but she didn't eat the ice cream because she was lactose-intolerant and would complain about its high price, insisting that her grandmother could make it better. This girl is crazy, I thought. Estee was good, but who could make ice cream better than Berthillon?

A SIMPLE REQUEST

One day, I mustered up some courage and marched into Berthillon with one request: Would the ice cream makers teach me their trade? "No," they swiftly responded.

I moved on to other ice cream shops in Paris—A La Mère de Famille, La Tropicale Glacier, Le Bac à Glaces—and got the same answer. No. No. No. Dejected, I went back to Estee. Why not see whether there was any merit to Max's words? One bite of Estee's ice cream cake and I was sold. Max's eighty-year-old grandmother did, indeed, make better ice cream than any shop I had visited.

I asked Estee to teach me, and to join me in opening a shop somewhere in Nice or Paris. She said she was too old, but pushed me to do it on my own. After a few months of flavor experimentation, trying different types of chocolates, fruits, and other ingredients, I moved my focus to milks—almond, rice, coconut, and others. I would try anything to get the perfect texture and consistency, and my determination was starting to pay off—people were loving what I created.

With Estee's quality-approval and blessing, I hosted my first party to showcase my frozen treats. The evening was an absolute success: I received rave reviews and even landed a few catering jobs.

A SCOOP OF CULINARY INNOVATION

I was thrilled my success was growing, but increasingly frustrated that Max couldn't partake in the ice cream revelry. There had to be some way I could make my desserts healthier and completely dairy-free, I thought. My mission was born.

I began testing and creating soy-based ice creams, which were, by default, healthier, lower in calories, and lactose-free. As I continued to experiment, I found that people loved both the interesting flavors—Kool-Aid, Peanut Butter and Jelly, Curry and Fig—and that they were healthier than regular ice cream. My experiments were a hit with Max, and the rest of her model friends too. But the best part? People couldn't tell that their dessert was dairy-free.

Despite the success of my new soy-based ice cream, I knew I should at least have a back-up plan (i.e., a college degree) if my ice-cream dreams didn't pan out. So instead of opening a shop right there in France, I headed home.

PHILADELPHIA CALLING

After my "summer" in Paris—which lasted two years—I enrolled at Temple University in Philadelphia and started looking for a job to pay for it all. Every restaurant I went, I was told that I could wash dishes. But I didn't want to be a dishwasher; I wanted to make desserts.

During that time, I began hanging around Piggy's, a popular barbecue restaurant in the city. One night at Piggy's, a huge commotion erupted in the kitchen, then spilled out into the dining room. There stood the owner and the cook, calling each other colorful names. And just like that, a position was opened and the owner needed to fill it—fast!

"Can anyone here cook?" he growled, frantically looking around the dining room. I saw an opportunity.

"I can," I replied eagerly. He waved me forward, as if I had volunteered to sacrifice myself. Others looked on with compassion. What did I sign up for?

Unfortunately, the restaurant changed hands soon thereafter and I was let go. But as luck would have it, I was offered a job as personal chef to one of Piggy's regular customers—he loved the ice creams and waffles I had added to the menu and wanted them in his own home. Now, this was the guy who would eat at a corner table by himself, who people always exhibited caution with when speaking to or walking by. It all made me a bit nervous, but the money was too good to refuse.

THE NEW BOSS

Mr. De Leon was a 6 foot, 5 inch (196 cm), 387-pound (176-kg) chain smoker who went through two packs of cigarettes a day and loved to eat. All he wanted was meat—90 percent of his diet was meat. He owned a nightclub and wanted his meals ready when he got home from work (pretty much any hour of the day).

My schedule was easy; Mr. De Leon would usually come home around the time I was getting ready for my first class of the day. Primarily, I would grill—steak, ribs, rabbit, venison, pork chops, and ham. He didn't want anything fancy. Every now and then, he'd request corn or mashed potatoes or some other side dish, but usually it was just meat and bread. And of course, dessert (ice cream being his favorite).

One day, Mr. De Leon began complaining of chest pains. I threatened to quit if he didn't go to the doctor. After several tests, he was diagnosed with high cholesterol and given a complete list of ailments that could develop (if they weren't developing already) as a result of his excessive weight and unhealthy lifestyle.

A NEW DIET FOR THE NEW BOSS

The doctor suggested a diet overhaul, which included cutting out some meat and eating more vegetables. I reassured Mr. De Leon that I would make any changes he needed and keep the food tasting just as great.

Then I suggested he become vegan. He didn't know what that was. I carefully explained the terms "vegetarian" and "vegan" to him.

Mr. De Leon laughed, saying that if he cut meat and dairy from his diet, he would die anyway. He had a million excuses.

I decided to end the discussion. I knew that Mr. De Leon was a competitive man by nature and would never back down from a challenge. "I'll do it too," I said. "Let's see which one of us can last longer as a vegan. I bet you $50,000 (£31,282) that I can stay vegan longer than you."

This was a win-win for me. I would either get Mr. De Leon to change his lifestyle and eating habits—and live years longer—or I would be a lot richer (and nobody could say I didn't try my hardest to help the man!). Plus, I was kind of excited to try being vegan after researching all the benefits of an animal-free diet. The data made sense. Being vegan was a good decision for anyone.

My plan worked. Mr. De Leon scoffed, said he had never lost a bet and wasn't going to start now. I assured him that I would be there and would make the food even better than before. I was totally invested in his change because I was doing it too—and I wanted to eat great food. I also revealed to him that he had been eating dairy-free desserts since I had started working for him. (He confessed that he really couldn't tell the difference). I had been making the recipes I created in France. I really thought their flavors were richer and truer than traditional ice creams, so why would I ever serve dairy again?

VEGAN FOR LIFE

It has been eight years since Mr. De Leon and I started our epicurean journey into the unknown—and we're both still going strong. We found so many great food choices in our vegan diet that we've never felt the need to stray. I am no longer Mr. De Leon's personal chef, but I will always be grateful for the interesting path I took because of him. Mr. De Leon did lose a good amount of weight and remains a vegan today, though he hasn't given up his old habits entirely—he still has quite a French fry addiction. His overall health has improved vastly, however, and both the chest pains and alarmingly high cholesterol are gone.

Turning the biggest vegan skeptic (and myself) into vegan proponents has been extremely rewarding. I didn't have more than $37 (£23) in my bank account when I placed that bet, but I had all the confidence in the world that I could create some terrific dairy-free desserts.

My belief and passion are continued today through Wheeler's Frozen Dessert Company, which I started in 2000, after finishing college. I began the company by selling ice cream out of a 1972 ice cream truck. I went to as many festivals and outdoor events as New England weather would permit. From there, my reputation—and number of catering jobs—began to grow. In 2007, I opened the first all-vegan ice cream parlor in Boston. Turns out there are throngs of people as passionate as I am about vegan ice cream!

This book showcases many of the recipes I offer in my shop, as well as recipes I've been inspired to create through my life adventures. I hope you enjoy making and tasting them as much as I've enjoyed creating them.

Introduction

Now, more than ever, it's extremely important to focus on global and human health. With high carbon dioxide emissions, murky BPA levels in plastics, dwindling natural resources, contaminated produce, and food-borne illnesses, it's no wonder people are turning to natural, organic diets and lifestyles.

Once shrouded in misconception, criticism, and aversion, vegan and vegetarian diets are becoming more and more appealing. Now approved and recommended by top doctors and physicians around the world, plant-based diets can contribute to a reduced risk of cancer, prevent and reverse cardiovascular disease, and eliminate the consumption of toxic chemicals found in meat, fish, and dairy products. In addition, following a vegan or vegetarian diet conserves natural resources and saves the lives of domestic and endangered animals.

Vegan and vegetarian diets are, by their very nature, healthy. This is because the bulk of the foods in such diets—whole grains, vegetables, fruits, beans, and nuts—are cholesterol-free, low in total fat and saturated fat, and rich in vitamins, minerals, and phytochemicals, which offer numerous health benefits. Many of these foods are also high in fiber.

VEGAN ICE CREAM: BEST IN TASTE AND NUTRITION

Contrary to popular myth, following a vegan diet is, in no way, restrictive or boring. Major supermarkets across the country carry plenty of meat and dairy alternatives. In fact, with the popularity of plant-based diets on the rise, more and more meat and dairy alternatives, including milk, butter, eggs, cheese, and ice cream, are showing up in the marketplace.

The recipes in this book provide a healthier way to enjoy frozen desserts traditionally high in calories, cholesterol, and saturated fat. To demonstrate this marvel, observe the nutritional breakdown (below) of our ice cream compared to leading commercial dairy brands.

Nutritional Breakdown: Vegan Ice Cream vs. All the Rest

SERVING SIZE: 4 OUNCES (APPROX. ½ CUP)	Calories	Total fat	Protein	Carbohydrates	Cholesterol	Sugars	Dietary Fiber
Wheeler's Frozen Dessert Company Vanilla	80	1.5 g	0 g	17 g	0 g	11 g	0 g
Häagen-Dazs Vanilla	289	19.3 g	5.4 g	22.5 g	129 mg	22.5 g	0 g
Cold Stone Creamery Vanilla Bean	264	15.4 g	4 g	25.7 g	60 mg	22.4 g	0 g
Ben & Jerry's Vanilla	240	16 g	4 g	21 g	75 mg	19 g	0 g
TCBY Vanilla Bean Frozen Yogurt	187	5.4 g	4.7 g	29.6 g	23 mg	24.9 g	0 g
Dairy Queen Vanilla Soft Serve	181	6 g	3.6 g	26.6 g	18 mg	23 g	0 g

GETTING TO KNOW YOUR INGREDIENTS

Containing zero cholesterol, 50 percent fewer calories, and 16 times less fat than some of the commercial, dairy brands of ice cream, the non-dairy ice creams featured in this book are an exciting, healthy, decadent treat suitable for people of all ages. My ice creams are substantially healthier than store-bought ice cream (including vegan store-bought ice cream) because they are made using fresh, all-natural ingredients and do not contain any preservatives or harmful additives. This translates into better tasting ice cream—without any worrisome "mystery" ingredients.

For a better understanding of the ingredients that go into these recipes, let's first take a look at the basic elements, and then examine the secondary players—such as fruits, nuts, and spices—that make these recipes shine.

The Main Players

Soymilk and soy creamer are two ingredients are essential to preparing vegan ice cream because they give the dessert its desirable, decadent consistency. Soymilk, often used as an alternative to dairy milk, is produced by soaking dry soybeans and grinding them with water. Soy creamer, much like dairy creamer, is thicker than milk and creates a silky texture.

The many different brands of soymilk and soy creamer offer a range of flavors, including plain, vanilla, chocolate, mocha, and chai. However, it's usually best to use the plain, full-fat versions of these products when making ice cream. That way, the taste comes from the spices and fresh fruit you add rather than from manufac-tured flavors.

Arrowroot is a gluten-free, flavorless powder often used as a thickener in cooking and baking. This herb, originating in tropical South America, is extracted from the *Marantha arundinacea* plant. In the sixteenth century, the Arawak people of the Caribbean favored it highly as a food with nutritious and medicinal value. In fact, it was often used to draw out poison from wounds inflicted by arrows, which may explain the origin of its name.

Arrowroot thickens at a lower temperature than flour or cornstarch, so it should be mixed with a cool liquid before being adding to warmer ingredients. When making vegan ice cream, arrowroot is first mixed with soymilk **(you will see this referred to as "arrowroot cream" in the recipes)**, then later added to the warm ice cream base. The powdered herb not only thickens the ice cream, but also prevents the formation of ice crystals and gives the dessert an appealing, glossy texture.

Sugar refers to a class of edible crystalline substances, of either monosaccharides (simple sugars) or disaccharides (a sugar carbohydrate composed of two mono-saccharides). Sugar, common in cooking and baking, also refers to sucrose, which is derived from plant sources such as sugarcane and sugar beets.

When purchasing sugar, pay attention to how it was refined. You don't want sugar processed using bone char as a filter. Instead, look for sugar processed with acti-vated carbon. This will usually be advertised as "kosher" or "parve" with indicators such as a U in a circle or a K on the packaging.

Vanilla, which is derived from orchids, is cultivated mainly in Madagascar, Indone-sia, and China. Because of the complex and extensive labor required to produce vanilla, the spice is second only to saffron in terms of cost. Highly valued for its flavor and bouquet, vanilla is widely used in baking, perfumes, and aroma therapy. Old medicinal literature also dubs vanilla as an aphrodisiac.

A Note About Milk

The recipes included in this book feature soy-based ice creams. However, we strongly encourage and recommend branching out and experimenting with other types of non-dairy milks. In addition to soymilk, non-dairy alternatives include almond milk, cashew milk, coconut milk, and rice milk.

For the ice cream flavors in our shop, we always offer more than one type of milk base to satisfy individual tastes and preferences. For example, some people prefer the sweet, nutty flavor that almond milk provides, while others may be allergic to nuts and therefore choose from our soy options.

When following any recipe, it is important to be familiar with your ingredients. Here's a handy guide to acquaint you with the different types of non-dairy milks commonly used in vegan ice cream.

Almond Milk and Cashew Milk

In the Middle Ages, nut-based milks often replaced cow's or goat's milks because the nut-based versions kept longer without spoiling. Today, many non-dairy and vegan recipes call for nut-based milk. That's because it is cholesterol-free and low in saturated fat. Plus, it contains fewer calories per serving than either dairy milk or soymilk. To produce this sweet, nutty beverage, grind up almonds or cashews (or both) and combine the nuts with water.

Coconut Milk

Recommended for ice cream recipes such as Sweet Curry Coconut (page 97) or Coconut Lemongrass (page 193), coconut milk is a delicious alternative to non-dairy milk. It can be thick or thin, depending on preparation. Thin coconut milk, made by pressing grated coconut through cheesecloth three or four times, is often used in soups and general cooking. Thick coconut milk, made by pressing coconut through cheesecloth once or twice, is recommended for rich, decadent ice creams. Note: You must refrigerate cans of coconut milk once they are opened, as they spoil easily.

Rice Milk

Rice milk is naturally sweetened through an enzymatic process that divides the carbohydrates in rice into sugars, namely glucose. Typically made with brown rice, it is non-dairy and non-allergenic milk, and often fortified with calcium, vitamin B12, and iron.

Soymilk

This milk, which originated in China, is produced by soaking dry soy beans and grinding them with water. Because soymilk is a stable emulsion of water, oil, and protein, it naturally has the same amount of protein as dairy milk. Plus, many manufacturers fortify their products with calcium. This low-in-saturated fat, cholesterol-free, non-dairy alternative has many benefits.

The First String: Fruits and Vegetables

Açai berries (pronounced ah-SAH-ee) have a sweet berry flavor with a subtle chocolate aftertaste. The berry contains extremely powerful antioxidants that have the potential to destroy human cancer cells. Açai palms grow mainly in the floodplains of Central and South America.

Apples are cultivated mostly in China and the United States. The health benefits of this fruit are incredibly diverse; according to research, apples may reduce the risk of cancer and heart disease, as well as assist in controlling cholesterol and weight. The fruit contains a good amount of vitamin C and dietary fiber. Apples are harvested in autumn and are commonly used in pies, ciders, cakes, crumbles, and other desserts, in addition to being eaten raw.

Apricots contain higher levels and wider varieties of carotenoids (antioxidants that assist in preventing heart disease, cancer, and high "bad" cholesterol levels) than any other food. Apricots grow in continental climate regions (those that are dry, and have hot summers and cold winters), but are also common in Mediter-ranean climates.

Avocados high in dietary fiber, potassium, and vitamin B6, are found in many cuisines and are especially common in vegetar-ian and vegan diets. Though the fruit is an excellent source of energy, its leaves, bark, skin, and pit are poisonous and should never be ingested.

Bananas are a valuable source of potassium and vitamins B and C, and are grown in more than 100 countries worldwide. Bananas are the largest of all herbaceous plants, and like flaxseeds, make an excellent egg substitute in vegan baking.

Blackberries are perennial fruits primarily grown in the pacific northwest of the United States. In fact, Oregon is the leading producer of blackberries in the entire world. Don't confuse these berries with black raspberries. Blackberries do not have hollow centers but do have numerous, large seeds. They also contain high amounts of vitamin K, manganese, and cancer-fighting antioxidants.

Blackcurrants are a rich source of vitamin C, contain more potassium than bananas, and are a good source of antioxidants and nutrients. Blackcurrants are often added to cocktails and wines for flavor.

Black raspberries are closely related to red raspberries, though the two differ in color, taste, and stem shape. These berries are often confused with blackberries, but they are a totally separate species. Black raspberries are high in the natural antioxidant anthocyanin.

Blueberries are native to North America, but also grow in Australia, New Zealand, and South America. Maine is the leading producer of blueberries in the United States. As such, its blueberry crops require about 50,000 beehives for pollination. Blueberries contain a diverse range of nutrients, including vitamins B6, C, and K, and dietary fiber.

Butternut squash is a winter squash similar to the pumpkin. Originating in Mexico, this squash is high in vitamins A and C and potassium.

Cantaloupe originated in India and Africa. It contains high levels of vitamin C and beta carotene, and like the vanilla bean, is processed to make extract and isolate superoxide dismutase, an enzyme associated with antioxidant defense. The cantaloupe was named after the commune Cantalupo in Sabina, Italy, a summer papal residence.

Carrots are extremely high in vitamins A and C and beta carotene. Carrots are grown worldwide and are included in many different cuisines.

Cashew fruit, which bears the more commonly known cashew nut, is native to northeastern Brazil, but is now widely grown in tropical climates. The cashew fruit is delicate and therefore, cannot be exported into the United States or Europe. It also has a short shelf life once picked from the tree.

Cherries are grown in twenty countries worldwide. Studies show that cherries, compared to other fruits, contain some of the highest levels of antioxidants. They also are a good source of beta carotene, vitamins C and E, potassium, iron, and fiber.

Coconuts are grown throughout the tropical world and are high in minerals such as iron, phosphorus, and zinc. They also contain a significant amount of water; one large coconut can produce up to a liter's worth. Additionally, coconut milk can be made by grating the coconut meat and mixing it with warm water. Nearly every part of a coconut palm can be used for something.

Cranberries, contrary to popular belief, do not grow in water. However, when the berries are ripe, the fields are flooded and a harvester drives through the beds to remove the floating fruit from the vines. Cranberries are an abundant source of antioxidants, protect against the formation of kidney stones, and may reduce the risk of urinary tract infections in females.

Cucumbers are technically fruit, though most people consider them vegetables. This fruit, pollinated by bees, has been cultivated for more than 3,000 years. Cucumbers are rich in vitamin A and are extremely low in calories.

Dates originated in the Middle East as early as 4000 BC. The fruit's four-stage ripening process is known in Arabic as the words *kimri* (unripe), *khalal* (full-size but crunchy), *rutab* (ripe and soft), and *tamr* (sun-dried on the tree). Dates are an excellent source of fiber.

Dragon fruit, also known as *pitaya*, has a unique appearance, with either a red or yellow colored spiny skin and pink or white soft flesh. The is taste often described as a mix between kiwi and Concord grapes. Dragon fruit is rich in minerals, fiber, and antioxidants.

Figs are one of the richest known plant sources of calcium and fiber. Although commonly considered fruit, figs are actually the flowers of fig trees, trees that have been cultivated for thousands of years, dating back to 9400 BC.

Goji berries, also known as wolfberries, are only commercially cultivated in China. They have been used in traditional Chinese medicine for almost 2,000 years, for their nutrients and antioxidants. The berries also contain eleven essential minerals, eighteen amino acids, and six essential vitamins.

Grapefruit, originally called the "forbidden fruit" of Barbados, is a hybrid of the pomelo and the sweet orange. Grapefruits are extremely high in vitamin C and contain significant amounts of vitamin B5. The United States is the leading producer of grapefruits worldwide.

Grapes are cultivated all over the world (there are more than 100 varieties) and contain beneficial antioxidants known as flavonoids, which give the fruit its vibrant purple color.

Guava, rich in vitamins A and C, dietary fiber, antioxidants, omega-3 fatty acids, and potassium, is considered a "super fruit." Plus, the whole fruit, from seed to rind, can be eaten. The more than 100 species of guava are grown in the tropical and subtropical regions of the world.

Honeydew melon, which originated in Persia, is part of the same botanical family as squash and cucumber. Honeydews are low in calories, but have a high amount of vitamin C.

Jackfruit, native to southern China, are the largest tree-borne fruit in the world. They taste similar to pineapple and are easily found in most Asian markets. Jackfruits are high in vitamins A and C, iron, and calcium.

Jalapeño peppers are medium-size chile peppers originating in Mexico. Much of their heat comes from their seeds and surrounding veins, so heat level can vary depending on preparation. Like all hot peppers, jalapeños contain antioxidants known as bioflavonoids, which act as powerful anti-inflammatories.

Key limes are more tart and bitter than their commercially available counterparts. These fruit, popular to use for pie, are native to southeast Asia and are a good source of ascorbic acid.

Lemons are citrus fruits good for an extensive array of culinary and non-culinary uses. Lemon trees bloom continuously year round, producing anywhere between 500 and 600 lemons annually.

Limes are high in dietary fiber, vitamin C, calcium, iron, and copper. The most common lime in the United States is the Persian lime (*citrus x latifolia*). The juice and zest from this tart cousin of the lemon are often used to flavor beverages and culinary dishes.

Lychees, native to southern China, have hard, nutlike shells and a delicately sweet inner pulp. Once picked from the tree, lychees deteriorate quickly and become inedible, giving the fruit its Chinese nickname *shanglin fu*, meaning "leaving its branches." Lychees are high in vitamin C.

Mangoes are high in dietary fiber, vitamin C, antioxidants, and carotenoids. There are more than 50 varieties of mangoes, the majority of which are native to India.

Mangoes can be difficult to cut. Try using this "hedgehog" method. Cut off the sides of the mango so you have four pieces (two big halves and two smaller pieces) of fruit and the thick, yellow pit. Discard the pit. Using a sharp knife, make horizontal slices into the flesh, but do not cut through the skin. Next, cut vertical lines. This should leave you with a checkerboard pattern. Now, using your thumbs, push the rind upward so the fruit pops away from it like a hedgehog extending its quills. Use a knife to cut off the chunks of mango.

Nectarines are similar to peaches, minus the fuzz. Gene studies of peach trees concluded that nectarines (*prunus persica*) evolved from a recessive peach gene, making it possible for nectarines to grow on peach trees, and vice versa.

Oranges are actually a type of berry because they have many seeds and derive from a single ovary. One serving of this nutritious fruit provides 75 percent of your daily vitamin C intake (based on a 2,000-calorie diet).

Papaya, the first fruit to have its genome studied and analyzed, is sometimes called the "tree melon" or "paw-paw." It is native to tropical North American lands and is the only food containing papain, a powerful enzyme that digests proteins and helps soothe upset stomachs.

Parsley is a biennial herb often used in culinary dishes. It is also sometimes planted in gardens to attract preda- tory insects away from more vulnerable plants.

Passion fruit, commonly used in desserts, drinks, and juices, is cultivated in many varieties. Passion fruit also contains significant amounts of vitamin A and phosphorus.

Peaches contain high amounts of potassium, vitamin C, and dietary fiber and are often used in salads, candies, and desserts, as well as eaten raw. They are cultivated in China, Europe, Iran, and the United States.

Pears grow in cool, temperate climates and are similar to apples in their pollination and cultivation. This sweet fruit is an excellent source of B-complex vitamins, as well as phosphorus and iodine. Pears are also one of the least allergenic fruits.

Pineapple is a sweet tropical fruit cultivated around the globe. It contains bromelain, a powerful digestive enzyme, as well as manganese and vitamin B1. Surprisingly, bats and hummingbirds are the most common pineapple pollinators.

Plums are a good source of dietary fiber, sorbitol, and vitamin C. This small, purple fruit is cultivated in the western United States, most notably in California.

Pomegranates were known as Punic apples to the Romans, and therein lies the root of their name. Pomegranate juice is well known for its cancer-fighting capabilities, as well as its effectiveness in reducing risk factors for heart disease. The fruit also is a great source of vitamins B5 and C and potassium.

Pumpkins are quite nutritious, containing high amounts of vitamin A and beta carotene. They are grown worldwide, usually planted in early July, and taste similar to other winter squash.

Raspberries, the tart berries grown in all temperate climates of the world, contain folic acid, iron, vitamin C, various B vitamins, and antioxidants. They have many antiviral and anticancer properties. The flowers of this berry's plant are major nectar sources for pollinating honeybees.

Rhubarb, indigenous to Asia, is famous for its earthy, sour flavor. For this reason, they are commonly sweetened with sugar and used in pies and other desserts. Rhubarb leaves are poisonous, but the stalks are edible and contain a good amount of calcium and dietary fiber.

Star fruit is native to the Tropics but is also commercially grown in Hawaii and southern Florida. Known for its star shape and its sweet, tart flavor, this fruit is an excellent source of vitamin C. Individuals with kidney problems should avoid star fruit, as it contains oxalic acid and can cause unpleasant or dangerous side effects.

Strawberries, as they are known today, actually developed through accidental hybridization of the North and South American species in the early eighteenth century. They are known for their unique seed location on the outside of the fruit. Strawberries are a recognized source of potassium, vitamin C, and dietary fiber.

Water chestnuts are grass-like plants grown for their edible stems, which can be eaten raw or cooked. Water chestnuts, which are native to China, are rich in carbohydrates and starch, potassium, dietary fiber, and copper.

Watermelons get their name from their high water content—there are 92 grams of water in each 100-gram slice. They are also significant suppliers of vitamins A and C. Their black seeds are roasted and eaten as a snack in many cultures.

Yams are starchy tubers native to Asia that contain high amounts of vitamins B6 and C, dietary fiber, and potassium. Most "yams" sold in the United States are actually sweet potatoes.

The Second String: Legumes, Nuts, and Seeds

Almonds, native to the Middle East, are extremely nutrient-dense, contain only one gram of saturated fat, and are a great source of vitamin E, magnesium, and potassium. The almond tree was one of the earliest cultivated trees known to man.

Black sesame seeds are great for many different foods and cuisines, and are often added to breads, bagels, crackers, and sushi. The oil that comes from these seeds is rich in manganese, copper, and calcium, and contains more antioxidants than any other edible oil.

Brazil nuts are native to South America, found on the banks of the Amazon, the Rio Negro, and Venezuela's Orinoco River. Brazil nuts are rich in selenium, protein, thiamine, and magnesium. Their taste is hard to describe, though some say it is reminiscent of coconut.

Carobs are legumes that date back to ancient Egypt. Often employed as a sweetener, carob seeds are also processed for use in cosmetics, paper, and tobacco curing. Carob powder and carob chips are commonly used in desserts and other confectionaries. Carob pods are rich in calcium and contain 60 percent fewer calories than chocolate.

Chestnuts are thin-shelled, sweet nuts that are high in water content and contain as much vitamin C as a lemon. There are four species of chestnuts: American, Chinese, European, and Japanese.

Cocoa powder comes from cocoa beans, which are harvested and used to make chocolate. Cocoa powder results from a three-step process: First, the dried, partially fermented seeds are ground. Next, 75 percent of the resulting cocoa butter is extracted. Finally, the resulting dark brown paste is re-dried and ground into powder. This becomes the unsweetened cocoa powder used in various cooking and baking recipes. Because most of the cocoa butter has been removed, cocoa powder is low in fat.

Flaxseed is an ancient crop that was a food source as far back as 3000 BC. High in protein and omega-3s, flaxseed is grown in two basic varieties: brown and golden. A tablespoon (7 g) of ground flaxseed mixed with water serves as an excellent egg replacement in vegan baking.

Hazelnuts are rich in iron, thiamine, and vitamin B6, and are a great source of protein. These nuts are commercially cultivated in Europe, Iran, and Turkey.

Oats are a type of grain grown throughout the temperate zones of the world. They are often used in cereals and breads, and are a great source of iron and dietary fiber.

Peanuts are legumes that were first domesticated in Peru. They are a rich source of protein and niacin, and contribute to brain health and circulation. Peanut butter is the number one use of harvested peanuts.

Pecans are an excellent source of protein and antioxidants. More than 90 percent of the fat found in these nuts is the unsaturated, heart-healthy fat. The name "pecan" originates from Algonquin and means "nut requiring a stone to crack."

Pine nuts, which are widely cultivated in Asia, Europe, and North America, are actually seeds extracted from some varieties of pine cones. They are an excellent source of protein and are often used in culinary dishes and salads.

Pistachio nuts have existed for more than 80 million years. When they ripen, their flesh changes from a light green to a yellow or red hue and their shells open with an audible pop. Pistachios are a good source of protein and dietary fiber.

Red beans, also known as adzuki beans, are the second most popular legume in Japan (after soybeans). Red beans are often boiled in sugar to create a paste, known as *an*, which is used in many Chinese dishes. Red beans are high in potassium and dietary fiber.

Walnuts are an important plant-based source of omega-3 fatty acids. There are many species of this nut, including Andean, Black, Brazilian, and California walnuts. Walnuts are beneficial to the brain, back, and skin, and in traditional Chinese medicine, are considered a tonic for the kidneys.

The Third String: Spices, Herbs, and Flowers

Anise, or aniseed, is a sweet and aromatic plant used in desserts, candies, and other confectionaries. Anise also is given as a remedy for colds and the flu and supposedly possesses aphrodisiac qualities; it is said that the chewing on anise seeds will increase desire.

Basil is prominent in Italian cuisine and is cultivated as a culinary herb, condiment, or spice. Studies show that basil is not only a potent antioxidant, but also wields powerful anti-aging, antiviral, and antimicrobial properties.

Brazilian pink pepper is not actually a pepper. In fact, it is a fruit but its berries are often sold as "pink peppercorns." Brazilian pepper is often used as an antiseptic and an antibacterial agent, though its fruit and leaves may be poisonous to small children. When used in moderation, this plant adds a peppery taste to food.

Cardamom, known for its intensely aromatic scent, is cultivated in two forms: Elettaria (green cardamom) and Amomum (black cardamom). This spice is common in Indian cooking, and also is helpful in treating digestion problems, congestion, snake bites, and tooth decay.

Cayenne pepper, named for the city of Cayenne in South America, is usually used to add spice to a dish. They also have been used medicinally to ease sore throats and cure stomachaches.

Cinnamon, native to India, is regarded as a highly prized essential oil. It contains antimicrobial agents and reduces blood sugar.

Dandelions, though considered weeds when found in gardens, are great in culinary dishes and as an herbal remedy. These flowers are especially important to bee colonies because their flowering indicates the start of honey season and an important source of nectar and pollen.

Eucalyptus, commonly known as a favorite snack for koala bears, dominates Australian tree flora. In fact, there are more than 700 species of eucalyptus. Though the plant can be eaten by humans, it's more often extracted into oil form.Eucalyptus oil is said to aid in decongestion and is found in many over-the-counter cough and cold lozenges, vapors, and ointments.

Ginger is a common cooking spice used in a variety of cuisines. It also has many medicinal uses, including reducing nausea and preventing the flu. Ginger contains vitamin B6 and magnesium and has a unique, distinct taste.

Ginkgo is a type of nut widely cultivated in China and used in Asian cuisine. It is said to enhance memory and concentration, and prevent vertigo. In large doses, it can be dangerous to children.

Ginseng is a sweet, licorice-flavored root that comes in two major types: American and Asian. According to traditional Chinese medicine, American ginseng promotes *yin* energy and possesses cooling properties. Asian ginseng promotes *yang* energy and possesses heating properties. Ginseng is thought to aid in the prevention of cancer and improve the immune system and blood circulation.

Jasmine, a flower popular for its aromatic scent, derives its name from the Arabic and Persian *yasmin*, meaning "gift from God" and is considered an aphrodisiac. It also is used in perfumes and teas.

Lavender has various culinary, medical, and aromatherapy uses. However, it also is a powerful allergen, so use it with caution. More than 30 species of lavender grow worldwide.

Lemongrass is a type of grass native to India. It is used most often in Thai and other Asian cuisines. Lemongrass is also a common ingredient in perfumes and soaps, and is thought to be a powerful aphrodisiac.

Licorice root is used to flavor many desserts, beer, candy, and soda. The root comes from the licorice plant, which is actually a legume. Licorice flavor is popular in the United Kingdom, Italy, and Spain, and is considered a decongestant and throat lozenge. Chewing on bits of licorice root is said to enhance love and lust.

Nutmeg is indigenous to southeast Asia and is used in many sweet dishes in Indian, Greek, and Middle Eastern cuisines. Large doses of nutmeg are toxic, especially to children.

Peppermint is actually a cross between water mint and spearmint. Often considered the world's oldest medicine, the plant dates back to 1000 BC and has been found in ancient Egyptian tombs. Its uses include easing headaches, fevers, indigestion, and throat and skin irritations.

Rose water, which was produced by medieval chemists, is the liquid portion of the distillate of rose petals. Rose water has a distinct flavor, most often found in South Asian and Middle Eastern cuisines. It is also used in perfumes and religious ceremonies. Iran produces the most rose water worldwide.

Rosemary is an excellent source of iron, calcium, and vitamin B6. Often called the dew of the sea, this plant is known to enhance memory and is thought to reduce the risk of cancer and strokes.

Saffron is the world's most expensive spice. It comes from the dried stigma of the saffron crocus, and is mostly cultivated in the Mediterranean, the Middle East, and California. Iran produces more than 95 percent of all the saffron in the world. Saffron is used as an anticarcinogen and has antioxidant-like properties.

Tarragon, which originated in Central Asia, is often used in French cuisine and to flavor vinegar, salads, soups, and pickles. In addition, it gives the Russian beverage *tarkhun* (a bright green carbonated soda) its taste. Tarragon is also known as Dragon's Wart.

Wasabi is a root vegetable that is commonly sold in paste or powder form. It is most often served with sushi, but can be used to spice up other dishes as well. Wasabi is cultivated in Japan and in the Pacific Northwest of the United States.

MEETING YOUR (ICE CREAM) MAKER

Now that you're familiar with the ingredients, let's get started on the "making" process. Ice cream makers are inexpensive—yet valuable—appliances that create decadent, homemade ice cream in any flavor you desire. Can't find Green Tea ice cream in your supermarket? No problem, if you have an ice cream maker. Just create it yourself!

Put simply, a domestic ice cream maker is a machine that makes small quantities of ice cream by churning the ingredients with a hand-crank or motor. There are a variety of ways to freeze the mixture. Most domestic makers partially freeze the mixture during churning, and then require that the ice cream be frozen completely in the freezer.

An ice cream maker's purpose is to simultaneously chill and churn the mixture to 1.) prevent the formation of ice crystals and 2.) produce a smooth, creamy texture.

What's Your Type?

There are two major types of ice cream makers: manual and electric. Both produce the same quality ice cream, yet each design has advantages and disadvantages.

Manual machines have an outer bowl and an inner bowl, with a hand-crank to churn the ice cream. The inner bowl holds the ice cream mixture; the outer bowl contains a freezing mixture of salt and ice. The churning of the hand-crank aerates and freezes the ice cream.

On the plus side, manual machines are somewhat inexpensive. However, they can be inconvenient and time-consuming. The salt mixture in the outer bowl gradually melts and must be replenished for each new batch of ice cream. In addition, stirring the ice cream with the hand-crank takes a good deal of energy and at least a half hour.

Electric machines do not require you churn the ice cream by hand. The electric motor and paddle do it for you. This no-labor aspect is one of the greatest advantages to electric machines. However, top-of-the-line versions can be expensive—hard to justify for those who only make ice cream occasionally.

Electric ice cream makers come in two varieties, which differ only in how the ice cream cools. Counter-top ice cream makers, the most popular homemade ice cream devices, feature a double-walled bowl (with a chemical freezing solution between the walls) and a motor that controls the stirring paddles. The entire bowl gets wrapped in plastic and frozen for 24 hours before the ice cream is made.

Once the bowl is frozen, it is ready for use. Most ice cream mixtures require 25 to 30 minutes of churning before they transform into a servable consistency, plus two to three more hours in the freezer before they harden enough to scoop.

With this type of maker, the freezing requirements make on-the-spot ice cream unattainable. Also, unless you own multiple bowls, you can make only one batch of ice cream at a time. Before you can start on another, the bowl must freeze for 24 more hours. On the plus side, this variety of electric ice cream maker can be purchased for $100 (£62) to $150 (£94).

Self-freezing electric ice cream makers, on the other hand, go for about $400 (£252). These makers don't require a prechilled bowl. Instead, after about five minutes, they are ready to start freezing the ice cream. Typically, the ice cream is ready to serve immediately after the churning process.

Unfortunately, in addition to their high cost, these ice cream makers are large and require a good amount of counter space. However, if price is no object and you have the room, these are the best machines for making multiple, large batches of ice cream with relatively little hassle.

Tips and Techniques for a Happy Relationship—with Your Ice Cream Maker

- Know your options. Ice cream makers have various bowl size options (e.g., 1.5 quarts [1.4 L], 5 quarts [4.7 L], etc.). Be sure to purchase one that has the capacity to make the quantity of ice cream you desire.

- Keep your ice cream maker clean and dry when it's not in use. Always follow the manufacturer's instructions for appliance maintenance.

- Chill ice cream mixture before placing it into the ice cream maker. This will help reduce churn and chill times, as well as retain flavor.

- Do not overfill the ice cream maker. If the bowl is too full, the ice cream will not aerate properly. Follow recipes whose yields are the same or less than your ice cream maker's capacity.

- Add flavor extracts (e.g., vanilla, maple, etc.) after the mixture has cooled, but before placing it in the ice cream maker.

- Add chopped ingredients (e.g., nuts, cookie dough, etc.) in the last few minutes of freezing. If the pieces are large or very hard, fold them directly into the ice cream by hand, once the churning is complete. This will prevent breaking the paddle or any other parts.

- Harden by transferring already-churned ice cream into a freezer-safe container and placing it in the freezer for two to three hours. Ice cream can be stored in the freezer in a sealed, plastic container for about two weeks.

- Never refreeze ice cream after it has melted. The flavor, texture, and overall quality will suffer significantly.

CHAPTER 1

Classic Flavors

My mentor and culinary coach Estee would always say, "The basics are like a mirror—they tell the truth." Her words convinced me that the best way to tell whether a person can cook is to try his or her basics. In my case, those basics are Vanilla and Chocolate.

My advice to anyone wishing to create delicious desserts would be to focus on the basics. Once you master them, making other desserts will be a cakewalk. When I was first learning how to make desserts, I would try to figure out ways to "cheat" and get through steps faster. It quickly became evident that careful consideration and the best ingredients will produce tastier results.

I tell everyone in my ice cream making classes to practice making Vanilla every day. Keep feeding your friends, loved ones, and neighbors. Believe me, the look in their eyes during their first couple bites will tell you just how they feel. Once you have a good command of Vanilla and Chocolate, the rest are easy.

Vanilla

Vanilla dates back to the Aztecs in Mexico. Today, vanilla ice cream is the #1-selling flavor worldwide. This rich, creamy version will keep everyone coming back for seconds.

1 cup (235 ml) soy milk, divided

2 tablespoons (16 g) arrowroot powder

2 cups (470 ml) soy creamer

¾ cup (150 g) sugar

1 tablespoon (15 ml) vanilla extract

In a small bowl, combine ¼ cup (60 ml) soymilk with arrowroot and set aside.

Mix soy creamer, remaining ¾ cup (175 ml) soymilk, and sugar in a saucepan and cook over low heat. Once mixture begins to boil, remove from heat and immediately add arrowroot cream. This will cause the liquid to thicken noticeably.

Add vanilla extract.

Refrigerate mixture until chilled, approximately 2 to 3 hours. Freeze according to your ice cream maker's instructions.

Yield: 1 quart (approximately 600 g)

SERVING SUGGESTION

"Spaghetti" Ice Cream with Brownie "Meatballs"

Who says you can't have ice cream for dinner? This fun, creative way to serve dessert is always a smash at birthday parties.

½ cup (60 g) all-purpose flour

⅓ cup (28 g) unsweetened cocoa powder

¼ teaspoon baking powder

¼ teaspoon salt

½ cup (110 g) non-hydrogenated, non-dairy butter

½ cup (170 g) agave nectar

2 tablespoons (15 g) ground flaxseed

6 tablespoons (90 ml) water

1 teaspoon (5 ml) vanilla extract

Preheat oven to 350°F (180°C or gas mark 4). Grease and flour a mini-muffin pan.

Sift together flour, cocoa powder, baking powder, and salt. Set aside.

In a large saucepan, melt butter. Remove from heat and stir in agave nectar, flaxseed, water, and vanilla. Mix in sifted dry ingredients and stir for 1 to 2 minutes, until you reach a batter-like consistency. Drop meatball-size mounds of batter into mini-muffin molds. Bake 25 to 30 minutes.

Yield: 12 meatballs

To make "spaghetti" ice cream, all you need is a pasta maker. Immediately before serving, push ice cream through a spaghetti maker onto a plate. Top with brownie meatballs.

Chocolate

Did you know that chocolate has more than 500 flavor components, double the amount found in vanilla and strawberry combined? This ice cream recipe is 100 percent classic and 100 percent delicious.

1 cup (235 ml) soymilk, divided

2 tablespoons (16 g) arrowroot powder

2 cups (470 ml) soy creamer

¾ cup (150 g) sugar

¼ cup (20 g) cocoa powder

½ cup (90 g) vegan chocolate chips

1 tablespoon (15 ml) vanilla extract

In a small bowl, combine ¼ cup (60 ml) soymilk with arrowroot and set aside.

Mix soy creamer, remaining ¾ cup (175 ml) soymilk, sugar, cocoa powder, and chocolate chips in a saucepan. Stirring frequently over low heat, melt chocolate chips, then bring to a boil. Once mixture begins to boil, remove from heat and immediately add arrowroot cream. This will cause the liquid to thicken noticeably.

Add vanilla extract.

Refrigerate mixture until chilled, approximately 2 to 3 hours. Freeze according to your ice cream maker's instructions.

Yield: 1 quart (approximately 600 g)

Tasty Tidbits

- Annual world consumption of cocoa beans averages approximately 600,000 tons (544,311 metric tons) per year. Consumers worldwide spend more than $20 billion (13£) per year on chocolate.

- A single chocolate chip provides sufficient food energy for an adult to walk 150 feet (46 meters).

Chocolate Chip

Vegan baking chips, available at most organic and health food stores, are a must for this recipe. For a more homemade, gourmet taste, try replacing pre-packaged chips with chopped up pieces of your favorite vegan chocolate bar!

1 cup (235 ml) soymilk, divided

2 tablespoons (16 g) arrowroot powder

2 cups (470 ml) soy creamer

¾ cup (150 g) sugar

1 tablespoon (15 ml) vanilla extract

1 cup (175 g) vegan chocolate chips

In a small bowl, combine ¼ cup (60 ml) soymilk with arrowroot and set aside.

Mix soy creamer, remaining ¾ cup (175 ml) soymilk, and sugar in a saucepan and cook over low heat. Once mixture begins to boil, remove from heat and immediately add arrowroot cream. This will cause the liquid to thicken noticeably.

Add vanilla extract.

Refrigerate mixture until chilled, approximately 2 to 3 hours. Freeze according to your ice cream maker's instructions. In the last few minutes of freezing, stir in chocolate chips.

Yield: 1 quart (approximately 600 g)

✳Variation: Chocolate Chocolate Chip
Why mess with a good thing? Because some people just can't get enough chocolate! To make Chocolate Chocolate Chip ice cream, simply add ¼ cup (20 g) cocoa powder to the cream mixture before heating it.

Mint Chocolate Chip

Mint was one of the earliest herbs discovered. In fact, it has been found in ancient Egyptian tombs dating back to 1000 BC. Add some fresh mint leaves to the finished product to give this refreshing treat some added color.

1 cup (235 ml) soymilk, divided

2 tablespoons (16 g) arrowroot powder

2 cups (470 ml) soy creamer

¾ cup (150 g) sugar

1½ tablespoons (23 ml) peppermint extract

1 tablespoon (15 ml) vanilla extract

¾ cup (130 g) vegan chocolate chips

In a small bowl, combine ¼ cup (60 ml) soymilk with arrowroot and set aside.

Mix soy creamer, remaining ¾ cup (175 ml) soymilk, and sugar in a saucepan and cook over low heat. Once mixture begins to boil, remove from heat and immediately add arrowroot cream. This will cause the liquid to thicken noticeably.

Add peppermint and vanilla extracts.

Refrigerate mixture until chilled, approximately 2 to 3 hours. Freeze according to your ice cream maker's instructions. In the last few minutes of freezing, stir in chocolate chips.

Yield: 1 quart (approximately 600 g)

Tasty Tidbit

- Peppermint extract may be combined with boiling water to make peppermint tea. If you're feeling under the weather, this drink is especially useful, as peppermint is known to soothe cold and flu symptoms.

✳Variation: Chocolate Mint-Chocolate Chip
If you're a true chocoholic, add ¼ cup (20 g) cocoa powder to the cream mixture before heating it to get a double dose of chocolate.

Chocolate Marshmallow

Vegan marshmallows are available in specialty health food stores and online. Or try making homemade marshmallows using a gelatin substitute.

1 cup (235 ml) soymilk, divided

2 tablespoons (16 g) arrowroot powder

2 cups (470 ml) soy creamer

¾ cup (150 g) sugar

¼ cup (20 g) cocoa powder

½ cup (90 g) vegan chocolate chips

1 tablespoon (15 ml) vanilla extract

1 cup (50 g) vegan marshmallows, chopped

In a small bowl, combine ¼ cup (60 ml) soymilk with arrowroot and set aside.

Mix soy creamer, remaining ¾ cup (175 ml) soymilk, sugar, cocoa powder, and chocolate chips in a saucepan. Stirring frequently on low heat, melt chocolate chips, then bring mixture to a boil. Once mixture begins to boil, remove from heat and immediately add arrowroot cream. This will cause the liquid to thicken noticeably.

Add vanilla extract.

Refrigerate mixture until chilled, approximately 2 to 3 hours. Freeze according to your ice cream maker's instructions. In the last few minutes of churning, add chopped marshmallows.

Yield: 1 quart (approximately 600 g)

Tasty Tidbit

- Marshmallows were once made from a plant called the marshmallow plant.

- Most marshmallows typically contain gelatin, an animal product. Thankfully, animal-friendly alternatives are available in most health food stores.

Green Fact

True or false? It is impossible for vegans to get vitamin B12 from their diets. False. Neither plants nor animals synthesize B12 naturally. Vitamin B12 is made from bacteria that contaminate animals and their feed. However, vitamin B12 is readily available in fortified breads, cereals, and soymilk. Be sure to check labels for vitamin and mineral content.

Rocky Road

The original Rocky Road recipe was created by William Dreyer, the founder of Dreyer's Ice Cream, to "give folks something to smile about in the midst of the Great Depression." This vegan version will do just that!

1 cup (235 ml) soymilk, divided

2 tablespoons (16 g) arrowroot powder

2 cups (470 ml) soy creamer

¾ cup (150 g) sugar

¼ cup (20 g) cocoa powder

½ cup (90 g) vegan chocolate chips

1 tablespoon (15 ml) vanilla extract

1 cup (50 g) vegan marshmallows, chopped

1 cup (110 g) chopped almonds (or walnuts [120 g], if you prefer)

In a small bowl, combine ¼ cup (60 ml) soymilk with arrowroot and set aside.

Mix soy creamer, remaining ¾ cup (175 ml) soymilk, sugar, cocoa powder, and chocolate chips in a saucepan. Stirring frequently on low heat, melt chocolate chips, then bring mixture to a boil. Once mixture begins to boil, remove from heat and immediately add arrowroot cream. This will cause the liquid to thicken noticeably.

Add vanilla extract.

Refrigerate mixture until chilled, approximately 2 to 3 hours. Freeze according to your ice cream maker's instructions. In the last few minutes of churning, add marshmallows and nuts.

Yield: 1 quart (approximately 600 g)

Tasty Tidbits

- Rocky Road typically makes the top-ten lists each year in ice cream flavor rankings.

- William Dreyer is also credited with inventing the flavors Toasted Almond and Peppermint Stick.

Tasty Tidbit

- The chocolate chip cookie was invented in 1937 by Ruth Wakefield at the Toll House Inn in Whitman, Massachusetts.

Chocolate Chip Cookie Dough

The best-made vegan cookie dough is indistinguishable from the non-vegan variety. Use it as soon as possible to prevent it from drying out.

For Cookie Dough:

½ cup (255 g) non-hydrogenated, non-dairy butter

¾ cup (180 g) agave nectar

1 cup (125 g) all-purpose flour

½ teaspoon salt

1 tablespoon (15 ml) vanilla extract

1 cup (175 g) semisweet vegan chocolate chips

¼ cup to 6 tablespoons (60 to 90 ml) water

For Ice Cream:

1 cup (235 ml) soymilk, divided

2 tablespoons (16 g) arrowroot powder

2 cups (470 ml) soy creamer

¾ cup (150 g) sugar

1 tablespoon (15 ml) vanilla extract

To make cookie dough: Blend butter and agave nectar in a large bowl until creamy. Stir in flour, salt, vanilla extract, and chocolate chips. Add water, 1 tablespoon (15 ml) at a time, until you reach a cookie dough consistency.

Roll small pieces of cookie dough into balls, and drop onto a cookie sheet covered in waxed paper. Place cookie sheet in freezer until needed.

To make ice cream: In a small bowl, combine ¼ cup (60 ml) soymilk with arrowroot and set aside.

Mix soy creamer, remaining ¾ cup (175 ml) soymilk, and sugar in a sauce-pan and cook over low heat. Once mixture begins to boil, remove from heat and immediately add arrowroot cream. This will cause the liquid to thicken noticeably. Add vanilla extract.

Refrigerate mixture until chilled, approximately 2 to 3 hours. Freeze mixture according to your ice cream maker's instructions. In the last few minutes of churning, add frozen cookie dough pieces.

Yield: 1 quart (approximately 600 g)

＊Variation: Cookies 'N Cream
To make this flavor, drop in 1 cup (225 g) chopped up sandwich-style cookies (instead of cookie dough) during the last few minutes of freezing.

Tasty Tidbit

- More than 1,000 years ago, the native people of Central and North America chewed their own version of "gum" made from the sap and resin found in trees.

Bubblegum

This tasty treat pops with flavor and fun! It's guaranteed to make you feel like a kid in a candy shop.

1 cup (235 ml) soymilk, divided

2 tablespoons (16 g) arrowroot powder

2 cups (470 ml) soy creamer

½ cup (100 g) sugar

1 tablespoon (15 ml) vanilla extract

¾ cup (170 g) bubblegum, finely chopped

In a small bowl, combine ¼ cup (60 ml) soymilk with arrowroot and set aside.

Mix soy creamer, remaining ¾ cup (175 ml) soymilk, and sugar in a saucepan and cook over low heat. Once mixture starts to boil, remove from heat and immediately add arrowroot cream. This will cause the liquid to thicken noticeably.

Add vanilla extract.

Refrigerate mixture until chilled, approximately 2 to 3 hours. Freeze according to your ice cream maker's instructions. In the last few minutes of churning, add chopped pieces of bubblegum.

Yield: 1 quart (approximately 600 g)

Green Fact

By eating vegan for a month, you can prevent a quarter-ton (227 kg) of soil from being eroded (by the meat production industry).

Cherries Jubilee

Created in 1897 for Queen Victoria, the famous cherries jubilee dessert is traditionally made with cherries and liqueur and served as a sauce over vanilla ice cream.

1 cup (235 ml) soymilk, divided

2 tablespoons (16 g) arrowroot powder

2 cups (470 ml) soy creamer

½ cup (100 g) sugar

1 tablespoon (15 ml) vanilla extract

1 cup (155 g) pitted cherries, chopped

1 cup (110 g) chopped almonds (or walnuts, if you prefer)

In a small bowl, combine ¼ cup (60 ml) soymilk with arrowroot and set aside.

Mix soy creamer, remaining ¾ cup (175 ml) soymilk, and sugar in a saucepan and cook over low heat. Once mixture begins to boil, remove from heat and immediately add arrowroot cream. This will cause the liquid to thicken noticeably.

Add vanilla extract.

Refrigerate mixture until chilled, approximately 2 to 3 hours. Freeze according to your ice cream maker's instructions. In the last few minutes of churning, add cherries and almonds.

Yield: 1 quart (approximately 600 g)

SERVING SUGGESTION
Roasted Pineapple Compote

"Compote" is fruit stewed or cooked in syrup, usually served as a dessert.

¼ cup (60 ml) dark rum

½ cup (75 g) golden raisins

3 tablespoons (42 g) non-hydrogenated, non-dairy butter, divided

1 pineapple, peeled and cut into slices

2 tablespoons (42 g) agave nectar

½ cup (120 ml) pineapple juice

In a saucepan over medium heat, heat rum for 1 minute or until bubbles appear along the pan's edge. Add raisins, stir, and remove pan from heat. Set aside until completely cool. Drain raisins, preserving rum and raisins separately.

In a large pan over high heat, melt 1 tablespoon (14 g) butter. Add half of pineapple slices and cook for 2 minutes, until fruit is golden. Turn over and cook slices on the other side, until golden. Transfer pineapple to a plate. Repeat with remaining pineapple and another tablespoon (14 g) of butter. Wash and dry pan.

Place pan over medium-high heat and add remaining 1 tablespoon (14 g) butter. When melted, add agave nectar and pineapple juice and cook for 1 to 2 minutes, until reduced by half. Add preserved raisins, 1 tablespoon (15 ml) reserved rum, and pineapple. Cook for 1 to 2 minutes, or until pineapple is heated through. Serve immediately.

Yield: 6 servings

Black Raspberry

Also known as the thimbleberry, the black raspberry gives this ice cream a decadent flavor and deep, purple color. Go ahead and treat yourself—it does have fruit, after all!

Tasty Tidbits

- Raspberries were praised in poetry by the Crusaders and used medicinally in medieval Europe.

- There are 200 varieties of raspberries grown worldwide.

1 cup (235 ml) soymilk, divided

2 tablespoons (16 g) arrowroot powder

1 cup (125 g) fresh black raspberries, divided

2 cups (470 ml) soy creamer

¾ cup (150 g) sugar

1 tablespoon (15 ml) vanilla extract

In a small bowl, mix ¼ cup (60 ml) soymilk with arrowroot and set aside.

Combine ½ cup (63 g) raspberries, soy creamer, remaining ¾ cup (175 ml) soymilk, and sugar in a blender and purée. Transfer mixture to a medium-size saucepan and cook over low heat. Once mixture begins to boil, remove from heat and immediately add arrowroot cream. This will cause the liquid to thicken noticeably.

Add vanilla extract.

Refrigerate mixture until chilled, approximately 2 to 3 hours. Freeze according to your ice cream maker's instructions. In the last few minutes of churning, add remaining ½ cup (63 g) raspberries.

Yield: 1 quart (approximately 600 g)

> ✳Variation: Strawberry
> Strawberries can easily be substituted in this recipe for another delicious classic. Simply replace the 1 cup (340 g) of fresh black raspberries with 2 cups (340 g) of sliced strawberries. Use half for the blended mixture and stir in other half at the end, in the last few minutes of freezing.

Tasty Tidbit

- Soft, chewy candy caramel is made by heating the sugar, corn syrup, vanilla, and coconut milk to no more than 248°F (120°C). Heating it to higher degrees creates hard caramel candy.

Caramel

This recipe is a dinner party favorite. If you have trouble finding vegan caramel, don't worry. It's easy to make yourself!

For Caramel:

1 cup (200 g) sugar

1 cup (235 ml) light corn syrup

¼ cup (55 g) non-hydrogenated, non-dairy butter

1 cup (235 ml) coconut milk

1 teaspoon (5 ml) vanilla extract

For Ice Cream:

1 cup (235 ml) soymilk, divided

2 tablespoons (16 g) arrowroot powder

2 cups (470 ml) soy creamer

½ cup (100 g) sugar

1 tablespoon (15 ml) vanilla extract

To make caramel: Slowly boil sugar, corn syrup, butter, and coconut milk until mixture reaches "thread" stage on a candy thermometer (235°F [113°C]). Remove from heat and add vanilla extract. Set aside.

To make ice cream: In a small bowl, combine ¼ cup (60 ml) soymilk with arrowroot and set aside.

Mix soy creamer, remaining ¾ cup (175 ml) soymilk, and sugar in a saucepan and cook over low heat. Once mixture begins to boil, remove from heat and immediately add arrowroot cream. This will cause the liquid to thicken noticeably.

Add vanilla extract.

Refrigerate mixture until chilled, approximately 2 to 3 hours. Freeze according to your ice cream maker's instructions. In the last few minutes of freezing, swirl in homemade caramel.

Yield: 1 quart (approximately 600 g)

Green Fact

You can prevent unnecessary waste by serving your ice cream in washable dishware or by using recyclable bowls and spoons.

Butterscotch

Butterscotch, often considered a royal confection, used to be one of Doncaster, England's main attractions. Get your own royal treatment by tasting this brilliantly creamy, indulgent flavor.

1 cup (235 ml) soymilk, divided

2 tablespoons (16 g) arrowroot powder

1 cup (225 g) packed brown sugar

2 tablespoons (28 g) non-hydrogenated, non-dairy butter

1 tablespoon (15 ml) vanilla extract

2½ cups (590 ml) soy creamer, divided

In a small bowl, combine ¼ cup (60 ml) soymilk with arrowroot and set aside.

In a 1- to 2-quart (0.9- to 1.9-L) pan, over medium heat, stir brown sugar, butter, and vanilla for 3 to 4 minutes, until butter melts, sugar dissolves, and mixture is bubbly. Pour in ½ cup (120 ml) soy creamer and whisk until smooth, then remove from heat. Set aside.

Mix remaining 2 cups (470 ml) soy creamer and remaining ¾ cup (175 ml) soymilk in a saucepan and cook over low heat. Once mixture begins to boil, remove from heat and immediately add arrowroot cream. This will cause the liquid to thicken noticeably.

Add butterscotch mixture to cream and whisk gently. Refrigerate until chilled, approximately 2 to 3 hours. Freeze according to your ice cream maker's instructions.

Yield: 1 quart (approximately 600 g)

Tasty Tidbit

- Butterscotch differs from caramel in that butterscotch derives its flavor from brown sugar, whereas caramel's flavor comes from caramelized (or slightly burnt) granulated sugar.

SERVING SUGGESTION
Grilled Plums

Grilled plums complement this ice cream flavor perfectly.

Vegan cooking spray

2 tablespoons (28 g) non-hydrogenated, non-dairy butter, melted

1 teaspoon (7 g) agave nectar

¼ teaspoon ground cinnamon

4 or 5 plums, halved and pitted

Coat an outdoor grill or stove-top grill pan with cooking spray and preheat to medium-high.

In a small bowl, combine melted butter, agave nectar, and cinnamon. Whisk lightly, then brush mixture over flesh side of halved plums.

Grill plums, flesh side down, for 5 minutes or until soft. Serve immediately.

Yield: 5 servings

Toffee

Toffee, a confection made with boiled molasses, is a unique treat that is sweet and sinfully delicious. You'll find it in two ways in this recipe—in the ice cream itself and in the candy bits throughout. For even more decadence, sprinkle some walnuts or pecans on top.

1¼ cups (295 ml) soymilk, divided

2 tablespoons (16 g) arrowroot powder

2 cups (470 ml) soy creamer

1 cup (150 g) brown sugar

¼ cup (60 ml) regular molasses

¼ cup (60 ml) blackstrap molasses (a darker, thicker molasses)

1 tablespoon (15 ml) vanilla extract

2 vegan toffee bars

In a small bowl, combine ¼ cup (60 ml) soymilk with arrowroot and set aside.

Mix soy creamer, remaining soymilk, brown sugar, and regular and blackstrap molasses in a saucepan and cook over low heat. Once mixture starts to boil, remove from heat and immediately add arrowroot cream.

Add vanilla extract.

Refrigerate mixture until chilled, approximately 2 to 3 hours. Freeze according to your ice cream maker's instructions. While mixture is churning, crush candy bars with a rolling pin, or break them up and pulse them in a food processor. During the last few minutes of churning, add crushed toffee pieces.

Yield: 1 quart (approximately 600 g)

❋Variation: Butter Toffee
This simple variation is a bit saltier than the original toffee recipe. To make Butter Toffee ice cream, use 1 cup (235 ml) rather than 1¼ cups (295 ml) soymilk, and replace blackstrap molasses with 3 tablespoons (42 g) non-hydrogenated, non-dairy salted butter.

Tasty Tidbits

- Blackstrap molasses is a byproduct of the process of refining sugar cane into table sugar. It is made from the third boiling of the sugar and is the least sweet of all types of molasses.

- In the nineteenth century, molasses was the most popular sweetener because it was much more affordable than refined sugar.

Peanut Butter

This all-natural ice cream has a smooth finish. Try making it with your favorite organic peanut butter. Note: Because the peanut butter acts as a binding agent, arrowroot powder is unnecessary for this recipe.

2 cups (470 ml) soymilk

¾ cup (195 g) peanut butter

½ cup (75 g) brown sugar

1 tablespoon (15 ml) vanilla extract

In a medium-size saucepan, combine soymilk, peanut butter, and brown sugar. Bring to a boil, then remove from heat.

Add vanilla extract.

Refrigerate mixture until chilled, approximately 2 to 3 hours. Freeze according to your ice cream maker's instructions.

Yield: 1 quart (approximately 600 g)

Chocolate Peanut Butter Swirl

This tantalizing chocolate ice cream with a peanut butter swirl is a favorite among kids and adults.

1 cup (235 ml) soymilk, divided

2 tablespoons (16 g) arrowroot powder

1 cup (235 ml) soy creamer

¾ cup (150 g) sugar

¼ cup (20 g) cocoa powder

½ cup (90 g) vegan chocolate chips

1 tablespoon (15 ml) vanilla extract

¾ cup (195 g) peanut butter

In a small bowl, combine ¼ cup (60 ml) soymilk with arrowroot and set aside.

Mix soy creamer, remaining ¾ cup (175 ml) soymilk, sugar, cocoa powder, and chocolate chips in a saucepan and cook over low heat. Once mixture begins to boil, remove from heat and immediately add arrowroot cream. This will cause the liquid to thicken noticeably. Add vanilla extract.

Refrigerate mixture until chilled, approximately 2 to 3 hours. Freeze according to your ice cream maker's instructions. In the last few minutes of freezing, swirl in peanut butter.

Yield: 1 quart (approximately 600 g)

Butter Pecan

Butter Pecan ice cream has been a favorite flavor for decades. One taste of this delicious, non-dairy version and you'll know exactly why.

- 1 cup (235 ml) soymilk, divided
- 2 tablespoons (16 g) arrowroot powder
- 2 cups (470 ml) soy creamer
- 3 tablespoons (42 g) non-hydrogenated, non-dairy butter
- 1 cup (150 g) brown sugar
- 1 tablespoon (15 ml) vanilla extract
- ½ cup (55 g) chopped pecans

In a small bowl, combine ¼ cup (60 ml) soymilk with arrowroot and set aside.

Mix soy creamer, remaining ¾ cup (175 ml) soymilk, butter, and brown sugar in a saucepan and cook over low heat. Once mixture begins to boil, remove from heat and immediately add arrowroot cream. This will cause the liquid to thicken noticeably. Add vanilla extract.

Refrigerate mixture until chilled, approximately 2 to 3 hours. Freeze according to your ice cream maker's instructions. In the last few minutes of churning, add chopped pecans.

Yield: 1 quart (approximately 600 g)

Tasty Tidbit

- The pecan tree is the only major nut tree that grows naturally in North America.

SERVING SUGGESTION
Chocolate Cups

This recipe offers a more creative way to serve your favorite dessert.

2 pounds (900 g) semisweet dark chocolate, chopped

Melt chocolate over a double boiler.

Place a 6- or 8-ounce (175- or 235-ml) drinking glass in center of 12 x 12-inch (30 x 30-cm) piece of cellophane and bring cellophane up walls of glass. Fold over rim, stuffing excess cellophane inside glass. This will make loose pleats. Repeat with 4 or 5 more glasses.

Hold rim of wrapped glass and dip it in melted chocolate, dipping as deep as you want chocolate cups to be. Place dipped cups upside down on a cookie sheet and place in refrigerator. Allow to harden for 1 hour or longer.

To remove cups: Using sharp scissors, trim cellophane just below the glass rim. Avoid touching chocolate with your fingers, as it will melt. Pull cellophane taut against the glass, holding the base of the glass with your left hand. With your right hand, gently loosen the chocolate cup from the glass. Snip off excess cellophane. Place cups in covered container in refrigerator until you need them.

Yield: 20 cups

Praline Pecan

Modeled after the indulgent candies known as pecan pralines, which are made from cream, sugar, and pecans, this recipe is great for holidays and banquets.

Tasty Tidbits

- There are more than 1,000 varieties of pecans.

- If you can't find evaporated soymilk in stores, make your own. To make 1 cup (235 ml) evaporated soymilk, bring 2½ cups soymilk (590 ml) to a boil over medium heat, stirring constantly until volume is reduced to 1 cup (235 ml). Cool and refrigerate.

For Praline:

2 cups (450 g) packed brown sugar

¼ cup (60 ml) water

¼ cup (60 ml) evaporated soymilk (see Tasty Tidbit)

1 cup (110 g) chopped pecan pieces and halves

2 teaspoons (10 ml) vanilla extract

3 tablespoons (42 g) non-hydrogenated, non-dairy butter, cut in pieces

For Ice Cream:

1 cup (235 ml) soymilk, divided

2 tablespoons (16 g) arrowroot powder

2 cups (470 ml) soy creamer

½ cup (100 g) sugar

1 tablespoon (15 ml) vanilla extract

To make praline: In a medium-size saucepan, combine brown sugar, water, and evaporated soymilk. Stirring constantly, bring to a boil over low heat. Cook until mixture reaches "soft ball" stage on a candy thermometer (235°F [113°C]). Remove from heat.

Stir in pecans, vanilla, and butter. Using a tablespoon, immediately drop onto waxed paper. Cool to room temperature and break into pieces. Set aside.

To make ice cream: Combine ¼ cup (60 ml) soymilk and arrowroot in a small bowl and set aside.

Mix soy creamer, remaining ¾ cup (175 ml) soymilk, and sugar in a saucepan and cook over low heat. Once mixture starts to boil, remove from heat and immediately add arrowroot cream. This will cause the liquid to thicken noticeably.

Add vanilla extract.

Refrigerate mixture until chilled, approximately 2 to 3 hours. Freeze according to your ice cream maker's instructions. In the last few minutes of freezing, stir in praline.

Yield: 1 quart (approximately 600 g)

Maple Walnut

Pairing the venerable walnut with the rich flavor of maple creates an ice cream variety that many call perfection.

1 cup (235 ml) soymilk, divided

2 tablespoons (16 g) arrowroot powder

1 cup (235 ml) real maple syrup

2 cups (470 ml) soy creamer

½ cup (100 g) sugar

1 tablespoon (15 ml) vanilla extract

1 tablespoon (15 ml) maple liqueur or dash of maple extract, if desired

¾ cup (90 g) coarsely chopped walnuts

In a small bowl, combine ¼ cup (60 ml) soymilk with arrowroot and set aside.

In a deep saucepan, bring maple syrup to boil and cook over medium-high heat, without stirring, for 10 minutes or until syrup reaches "soft ball" stage on a candy thermometer (234°F [112°C]). Set aside.

Mix soy creamer, remaining ¾ cup (175 ml) soymilk, and sugar in a saucepan and cook over low heat. Once mixture starts to boil, remove from heat and immediately add arrowroot cream. This will cause the liquid to thicken noticeably.

Add vanilla extract. Blend in maple syrup mixture and maple liqueur, if desired.

Refrigerate mixture until chilled, approximately 2 to 3 hours. Freeze according to your ice cream maker's instructions. In the last few minutes of freezing, stir in chopped walnuts.

Yield: 1 quart (approximately 600 g)

Tasty Tidbit

- The walnut appears in Greek mythology, in the story of Carya, with whom the god Dionysus fell in love. When Carya died, Dionysus transformed her into a walnut tree. The goddess Artemis carried the news to Carya's father and he commanded that a temple be built in her memory. Its columns, sculpted in wood in the form of young women, were called caryatides, or nymphs of the walnut tree.

✻Variation: Maple Pecan or Maple Almond
Though walnuts are the traditional nut used in this ice cream, feel free to substitute an equal amount of pecans or almonds (or a combination of all three) for the walnuts..

Almond

Almonds are rich in protein, vitamin E, and other minerals. So go ahead, have two scoops!

Tasty Tidbits

- Almonds have the highest protein content of any nut.
- California is the only state in the United States that can successfully grow almonds.

1 cup (235 ml) almond milk, divided

2 tablespoons (16 g) arrowroot powder

2 cups (470 ml) soy creamer

¾ cup (150 g) sugar

1 tablespoon (15 ml) vanilla extract

1 tablespoon (15 ml) almond extract

¾ cup (110 g) roasted almonds, chopped coarsely

In a small bowl, combine ¼ cup (60 ml) almond milk with arrowroot and set aside.

Mix remaining ¾ cup (175 ml) almond milk, soy creamer, and sugar in a saucepan and cook over low heat. Once mixture begins to boil, remove from heat and immediately add arrowroot cream. This will cause the liquid to thicken noticeably.

Stir in vanilla and almond extracts.

Refrigerate mixture until chilled, approximately 2 to 3 hours. Freeze according to your ice cream maker's instructions. In the last few minutes of churning, add chopped almonds.

Yield: 1 quart (approximately 600 g)

SERVING SUGGESTION
Pear Purée

A purée is food that has gone through a sieve, blender, or the like and become the consistency of a soft paste or thick liquid. This light, crystal pear purée is delicious served atop a generous scoop of ice cream.

15 to 18 Anjou pears, peeled and cut into 8 pieces

½ cup (120 ml) water

⅔ cup (160 ml) pear vinegar (available at specialty or health food stores, or online)

⅓ cup (115 g) agave nectar

⅔ cup (160 ml) pear liqueur or brandy, such as Poire William

Simmer pears and water in large saucepan, stirring occasionally for 40 minutes or until pears are soft. Blend until smooth. Return to saucepan.

Mix in vinegar and agave nectar. Stirring frequently, simmer for 40 minutes or until reduced by one third and thickened to consistency of applesauce. Mix in pear liqueur.

Serve at room temperature.

Yield: 5 cups (1180 ml)

Pistachio

This pistachio recipe is great for those who want something a little nutty and sophisticated. Once you try it, you'll be hooked.

½ cup (60 g) plus 2 tablespoons (14 g) shelled pistachio nuts, divided

2 tablespoons (28 ml) corn syrup

1 cup (235 ml) soy creamer

½ cup (100 g) sugar

½ teaspoon almond extract

½ teaspoon vanilla extract

¼ teaspoon salt

1 cup (235 ml) soymilk

Place ½ cup (60 g) pistachio nuts in blender with corn syrup. Blend until smooth.

In a small bowl, whisk soy creamer and sugar together until sugar dissolves. Add mixture to blender and blend until smooth. Stir in almond and vanilla extracts, salt, and soymilk.

Refrigerate mixture until chilled, approximately 2 to 3 hours. Freeze according to your ice cream maker's instructions. In the last few minutes of churning, drop in remaining 2 tablespoons (14 g) pistachio nuts.

Yield: 1 quart (approximately 600 g)

Tasty Tidbits

- Humans have eaten pistachio nuts for at least 9,000 years. Pistachios are one of only two nuts mentioned in the Bible. The other is the almond.

- Pistachio orchards bear nuts in alternate cycles, meaning the trees produce a heavy amount of nuts one year and a light amount the next.

Green Fact

True or false? It is impossible for vegans to obtain adequate amounts of calcium since they don't drink milk. False. Tofu, leafy greens, watercress, dried fruit, seeds, and nuts are all great sources of calcium. In addition, many grains and soymilk brands are fortified with calcium.

Coffee

This sophisticated flavor pairs wonderfully well with our Black Raspberry ice cream (see page 46) and Almond Biscotti.

1 cup (235 ml) soymilk, divided

2 tablespoons (16 g) arrowroot powder

2 cups (470 ml) soy creamer

¾ cup (175 ml) fresh, strong coffee

¾ cup (150 g) sugar

1 tablespoon (15 ml) vanilla extract

In a small bowl, combine ¼ cup (60 ml) soymilk with arrowroot. Set aside.

Mix soy creamer, remaining ¾ cup (175 ml) soymilk, coffee, and sugar in a saucepan and cook over low heat. Once mixture begins to boil, remove from heat and add arrowroot cream. This will cause the liquid to thicken noticeably. Add vanilla extract.

Refrigerate mixture until chilled, approximately 2 to 3 hours. Freeze according to your ice cream maker's instructions.

Yield: 1 quart (approximately 600 g)

Tasty Tidbit

- It said that Christopher Columbus relied on biscotti, which have a long shelf life, as a ration on board his sailing fleets. The cookies were ideal for sailors, soldiers, and fishermen on long voyages.

SERVING SUGGESTION

Almond Biscotti

3 tablespoons (23 g) ground flaxseed

9 tablespoons (135 ml) water

1 teaspoon (5 ml) vanilla extract

½ teaspoon almond extract

¼ cup plus 2 tablespoons (127 g) agave nectar

2 cups (250 g) all-purpose flour

1 teaspoon (4.6 g) baking powder

⅛ teaspoon salt

1 cup (145 g) whole blanched almonds, toasted and chopped

Preheat oven to 350° F (180° C or gas mark 4). Line a baking sheet with parchment paper.

In a small bowl, whisk flaxseed, water, and vanilla and almond extracts until slightly frothy and gelatinous. Stir in agave nectar.

In the bowl of an electric mixer, combine flour, agave nectar, baking powder, and salt. Gradually add flaxseed mixture to flour mixture and beat until a dough forms, adding almonds about halfway through.

Transfer dough to a lightly floured surface and divide in half. Shape each half into a log about 10 inches (25 cm) long and 2 inches (5 cm) wide. Slide logs onto the prepared baking sheet, spacing them 3 inches (7.5 cm) apart, and bake for 22 to 25 minutes, or until slightly firm to the touch. Cool on a wire rack for about 5 minutes. While they're cooling, reduce oven to 300° F (150° C or gas mark 2).

Transfer logs to a cutting board. Using a serrated knife, cut logs into ½-inch (1-cm) thick slices on the diagonal. Arrange evenly on baking sheet. Bake 10 minutes, turn over, and bake another 10 minutes or until firm to the touch. Remove from oven and let cool completely.

Yield: 40 biscotti

CHAPTER 2

Fruity Flavors

Farmers' markets are great places to find local, fresh fruit and vegetables. Locally grown produce is a necessity for my recipes because they bring out flavors and colors unmatched by trucked-in or flown-in goods.

With local fruit, I know it was picked at its peak and brought directly to be sold. I can chat with the farmer, meet the person who actually planted the seeds and tilled the land.

Plus, buying locally benefits the community and conserves natural resources. The food isn't shipped hundreds of miles by truck or plane, so the fruits and vegetables retain a superb quality and conserve oil and reduce carbon emissions.

In the end, the choice is up to you. I always go local.

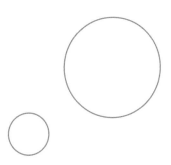

Tasty Tidbits

- Blueberries are native only to North America.

- Blueberries differ from bilberries and huckleberries in that blueberries have white or greenish flesh, while the latter two are purple throughout.

Blueberry

Sweet and antioxidant-rich blueberries rank high on the list of fruits that can help destroy free radicals, the molecules that play a role in aging and disease. Enjoy this invigorating ice cream with fresh fruit on the side.

1 cup (235 ml) soymilk, divided

2 tablespoons (16 g) arrowroot powder

1 cup (145 g) blueberries

¾ cup (150 g) sugar, divided

Splash of lemon juice

2 cups (470 ml) soy creamer

1 tablespoon (15 ml) vanilla extract

In a small bowl, combine ¼ cup (60 ml) soymilk with arrowroot and set aside.

Mix blueberries, ¼ cup (50 g) sugar, and lemon juice in a small saucepan. Heat until boiling and some blueberries have burst. Set aside.

Mix soy creamer, remaining ¾ cup (175 ml) soymilk, and remaining ½ cup (100 g) sugar in a saucepan and cook over low heat. Once mixture begins to boil, remove from heat and immediately add arrowroot cream. This will cause the liquid to thicken noticeably.

Add vanilla extract and blueberry sauce you created earlier.

Refrigerate mixture until chilled, approximately 2 to 3 hours. Freeze according to your ice cream maker's instructions.

Yield: 1 quart (approximately 600 g)

✱Variation: Berries Galore

This recipe works well with many berry varieties. Simply follow the instructions for Blueberry ice cream, substituting in 1 cup of blackberries (145 g), raspberries (125 g), or cranberries (100 g).

Banana

Horticulturalists speculate that the banana was the world's first fruit. As an ice cream flavor, it is sure to stick around for centuries more.

3 bananas, peeled and sliced

1 cup (235 ml) soymilk, divided

2 tablespoons (16 g) arrowroot powder

2 cups (470 ml) soy creamer

½ cup (100 g) sugar

1 tablespoon (15 ml) vanilla extract

In a food processor, purée bananas and set aside.

In a small bowl, combine ¼ cup (60 ml) soymilk with arrowroot and set aside.

Mix soy creamer, remaining ¾ cup (175 ml) soymilk, bananas, and sugar in a saucepan and cook over low heat. Once mixture begins to boil, remove from heat and immediately add arrowroot cream. This will cause the liquid to thicken noticeably.

Add vanilla extract.

Refrigerate mixture until chilled, approximately 2 to 3 hours. Freeze according to your ice cream maker's instructions.

Yield: 1 quart (approximately 600 g)

Tasty Tidbits

- Bananas grow mostly in tropical climates, but can also flourish in geyser-heated soil, like in Iceland.

- A cluster of bananas, which consists of 10 to 20 of the fruit, is called a "hand." The individual bananas are called "fingers."

SERVING SUGGESTION

Crunchy Chocolate Balls

These crunchy treats are a fantastic complement to some smooth Banana ice cream.

¼ cup (55 g) non-hydrogenated, non-dairy butter

1 cup (340 g) agave nectar

½ cup (40 g) cocoa powder

½ cup (120 ml) soymilk

3 cups (240 g) oats

1 cup (80 g) shredded coconut

1 teaspoon (5 ml) vanilla extract

Grease a baking tray. Combine butter, agave nectar, cocoa powder, and soymilk in a large saucepan. Cook on medium heat until mixture starts boiling, stirring continuously. Put on low heat and let boil for exactly 5 minutes, stirring once or twice if necessary.

Remove saucepan from heat. Stir in oats, coconut, and vanilla. Using two teaspoons, form balls with the mixture and place on baking tray. Put in refrigerator to set, 1 to 2 hours or until chocolate hardens.

Yield: 15 balls

Fig

Of all common fruits, figs have the highest mineral content. This dessert is perfect for a midsummer night's treat!

1 cup (235 ml) soymilk, divided

2 tablespoons (16 g) arrowroot powder

20 fresh figs, chopped, or 1 cup (320 g) fig preserves

½ cup (120 ml) water

1 cup (200 g) sugar, divided

2 cups (470 ml) soy creamer

Pinch of salt

1 teaspoon (5 ml) lemon juice

1 tablespoon (15 ml) vanilla extract

In a small bowl, combine ¼ cup (60 ml) soymilk with arrowroot and set aside.

Remove stems from figs and chop fruit into small pieces. Place figs in a saucepan with water and ¼ cup (50 g) sugar. Cook mixture over medium heat, stirring occasionally, until it becomes thick, soft, and jam-like.

Combine fig mixture, soy creamer, remaining ¾ cup (175 ml) soymilk, and remaining ¾ cup (150 g) sugar in a saucepan and cook over low heat. Add salt and lemon juice. Once mixture begins to boil, remove from heat and immediately add arrowroot cream. This will cause the liquid to thicken noticeably.

Add vanilla extract.

Refrigerate mixture until chilled, approximately 2 to 3 hours. Freeze according to your ice cream maker's instructions.

Yield: 1 quart (approximately 600 g)

Tasty Tidbits

• Figs come in an array of colors—yellow, red, brown, and purple, too!

• Fresh figs do not keep well and can be stored in the refridgerator for only 1 to 2 days.

Green Fact

An important part of buying locally means purchasing fruits and vegetables when they are in season. This eliminates environmental damage caused by shipping.

Tasty Tidbit

- A nectarine is a fuzz-less variety of a peach, and the two belong to the same species. Genetically speaking, the fuzzless skin of the nectarine is a reces-sive gene; the fuzz-full skin of the peach is a dominant gene.

Nectarine

The nectarine is smaller than its cousin, the peach, and has a noticeable pink tinge to its flesh. Sprinkle cinnamon on top of the ice cream to add a delicious note to this dessert.

1 cup (235 ml) soymilk, divided

2 tablespoons (16 g) arrowroot powder

4 to 5 nectarines, chopped, divided

2 cups (470 ml) soy creamer

¾ cup (150 g) sugar

1 tablespoon (15 ml) vanilla extract

In a small bowl, combine ¼ cup (60 ml) soymilk with arrowroot and set aside.

Purée half of chopped nectarines in a food processor.

Combine puréed nectarines, soy creamer, remaining ¾ cup (175 ml) soymilk, and sugar in a saucepan and cook over low heat. Once mixture begins to boil, remove from heat and immediately add arrowroot cream. This will cause the liquid to thicken noticeably.

Add vanilla extract.

Refrigerate mixture until chilled, approximately 2 to 3 hours. Freeze according to your ice cream maker's instructions. In the last few minutes of freezing, stir in remaining chopped nectarines.

Yield: 1 quart (approximately 600 g)

SERVING SUGGESTION
Raspberry Syrup

Drizzled over any ice cream, this syrup is a sweet and flavorful final touch.

2½ tablespoons (35 ml) water

1½ tablespoons (20 g) sugar

1 cup (125 g) raspberries

To make the sugar syrup: Combine water and sugar and cook on low heat until simmering, 2 to 3 minutes.

Carefully wash raspberries, purée in a blender, and place through a sieve to prevent any seeds from getting into syrup. Combine with sugar syrup and continue blending until smooth. Remove from heat and serve immediately (or refrigerate for later use).

Yield: 6 servings

Plum

This recipe is perfect for late summer. Look for fresh, organic plums to turn this crisp, light ice cream a beautiful hue.

1 cup (235 ml) soymilk, divided

2 tablespoons (16 g) arrowroot powder

6 purple or black plums, diced

2 cups (470 ml) soy creamer

¾ cup (150 g) sugar

1 tablespoon (15 ml) vanilla extract

In a small bowl, combine ¼ cup (60 ml) soymilk with arrowroot and set aside.

Purée plums in a food processor until smooth; strain and discard skins.

Combine puréed plums, soy creamer, remaining ¾ cup (175 ml) soymilk, and sugar in a saucepan and cook over low heat. Once mixture begins to boil, remove from heat and immediately add arrowroot cream. This will cause the ice cream to thicken noticeably.

Add vanilla extract.

Refrigerate mixture until chilled, approximately 2 to 3 hours. Freeze according to your ice cream maker's instructions.

Yield: 1 quart (approximately 600 g)

Tasty Tidbits

- Plums grown in Britain actually originated in Damascus, Persia, and Syria.

- Just as individuals have unique human fingerprints, each plum variety has a unique plum stone.

Green Fact

It is important to buy locally grown food. After fruits and vegetables are harvested, they begin to lose their nutrients. The less time it takes for the food to reach your plate, the more nutritious it is.

Tasty Tidbits

- Oranges are one of the few fruits that will not overripen if left on the tree.

- The orange is the most commonly grown tree fruit in the world.

Orange

Refreshing and packed with vitamin C, this citrus creation is a bowlful of health. Take your dish one step further and top it with our Orange-Basil Marinated Pineapple, and no one will argue when you say you're eating ice cream to boost your daily fruit intake!

1 cup (235 ml) soymilk, divided

2 tablespoons (16 g) arrowroot powder

3 large navel oranges

2 cups (470 ml) soy creamer

¾ cup (150 g) sugar

1 tablespoon (15 ml) vanilla extract

1 tablespoon (15 ml) almond extract

In a small bowl, combine ¼ cup (60 ml) soymilk with arrowroot and set aside.

Finely grate 2 tablespoons (12 g) zest from oranges, then halve oranges and squeeze enough juice to measure 1 cup (235 ml). Discard oranges.

Combine zest, orange juice, soy creamer, remaining ¾ cup (175 ml) soymilk, and sugar in a saucepan and cook over low heat. Once mixture begins to boil, remove from heat and immediately add arrowroot cream. This will cause the liquid to thicken noticeably.

Add vanilla and almond extracts.

Refrigerate mixture until chilled, approximately 2 to 3 hours. Freeze according to your ice cream maker's instructions.

Yield: 1 quart (approximately 600 g)

SERVING SUGGESTION

Orange-Basil Marinated Pineapple

Served alongside our bright Orange ice cream, this gourmet dish is great after any meal.

½ cup (120 ml) olive oil, divided

2 cloves garlic, minced

Juice of 2 oranges

½ tablespoon chopped fresh basil leaves

1 tablespoon (12.5 g) sugar

¼ teaspoon salt

1 pineapple

To prepare marinade, heat 2 tablespoons (28 ml) oil in a saucepan and add garlic. Sauté over medium heat for 4 to 5 minutes, until translucent. Pour into a medium-size bowl and add remaining oil, orange juice, basil, sugar, and salt. Stir to combine.

Carefully skin and cut pineapple into slices and lay flat in a glass baking dish. Pour marinade atop pineapple to coat and place in refrigerator for a few hours.

Yield: 8 servings

Grapefruit

This healthy treat is perfect for brunch or a late-afternoon snack. But be prepared, the ice cream has much of the same tartness as the fruit itself.

1 cup (235 ml) soymilk, divided

2 tablespoons (16 g) arrowroot powder

3 large grapefruits

2 cups (470 ml) soy creamer

¾ cup (150 g) sugar

1 tablespoon (15 ml) vanilla extract

In a small bowl, combine ¼ cup (60 ml) soymilk with arrowroot and set aside.

Finely grate 2 tablespoons (12 g) zest from grapefruits, then halve and squeeze 1 cup (235 ml) juice. Discard remaining grapefruit.

Combine zest, grapefruit juice, soy creamer, remaining ¾ cup (175 ml) soymilk, and sugar in a saucepan and cook over low heat. Once mixture begins to boil, remove from heat and immediately add arrowroot cream. This will cause the liquid to thicken noticeably.

Add vanilla extract.

Refrigerate mixture until chilled, approximately 2 to 3 hours. Freeze according to your ice cream maker's instructions.

Yield: 1 quart (approximately 600 g)

Tasty Tidbits

- The grapefruit is a cross between a sweet orange and a pomelo.

- Drinking three 6-ounce (175-ml) glasses of grapefruit juice a day has been shown to reduce the activity of an enzyme that activates the cancer-causing chemicals found in tobacco smoke.

Green Fact

Studies show that animal protein is more likely to cause cancer than any chemical carcinogen.

Tasty Tidbits

- There are two types of honeydew melons: one with green flesh, the other with orange flesh.

- Honeydew is one of the few melons that continues to ripen once picked.

Honeydew

With such a sweet flavor, it's no wonder this fruit is also known as the "temptation melon." When fully ripe, the flesh will be a brilliant white hue. Serve this ice cream after dinner, with fresh fruit and nuts.

1 cup (235 ml) soymilk, divided

2 tablespoons (16 g) arrowroot

½ very ripe honeydew melon, cut into chunks

½ cup (100 g) sugar

1 teaspoon (5 ml) freshly squeezed lime juice

2 cups (470 ml) soy creamer

1 tablespoon (15 ml) vanilla extract

In a small bowl, combine ¼ cup (60 ml) soymilk with arrowroot and set aside.

In a food processor, blend honeydew, sugar, and lime juice until smooth.

Combine blended honeydew mixture, soy creamer, and remaining ¾ cup (175 ml) soymilk in a saucepan and cook over low heat. Once mixture begins to boil, remove from heat and immediately add arrowroot cream. This will cause the liquid to thicken noticeably.

Add vanilla extract.

Refrigerate mixture until chilled, approximately 2 to 3 hours. Freeze according to your ice cream maker's instructions.

Yield: 1 quart (approximately 600 g)

✻Variation: Cantaloupe

High in beta carotene and vitamin C, cantaloupes are great to use in dessert dishes. To make Cantaloupe ice cream, simply substitute one large, ripe cantaloupe for the honeydew melon.

Pomegranate

Delight your taste buds with this tart creation. To avoid a mess (and dying your hands pink from the seeds of a fresh pomegranate), try using organic pomegranate juice. It packs the same vitamins and antioxidants, and the flavor is unbeatable.

1 cup (235 ml) soymilk, divided

2 tablespoons (16 g) arrowroot powder

1 cup (235 ml) organic pomegranate juice

2 cups (470 ml) soy creamer

¾ cup (150 g) sugar

1 tablespoon (15 ml) vanilla extract

In a small bowl, combine ¼ cup (60 ml) soymilk with arrowroot and set aside.

Combine pomegranate juice, soy creamer, remaining ¾ cup (175 ml) soymilk, and sugar in a saucepan and cook over low heat. Once mixture begins to boil, remove from heat and immediately add arrowroot cream. This will cause the liquid to thicken noticeably.

Add vanilla extract.

Refrigerate mixture until chilled, approximately 2 to 3 hours. Freeze according to your ice cream maker's instructions.

Yield: 1 quart (approximately 600 g)

Rhubarb

Also known as the "pie fruit" for its regular appearance in the dessert, rhubarb has a distinctly tart taste and aroma. Sprinkle sugar or slices of ginger on top if you find the flavor strong.

1 cup (235 ml) soymilk, divided

2 tablespoons (16 g) arrowroot

1 pound (455 g) rhubarb, cut into ½-inch (1-cm) pieces

1½ cups (300 g) sugar, divided

2 cups (470 ml) soy creamer

1 tablespoon (15 ml) vanilla extract

In a small bowl, combine ¼ cup (60 ml) soymilk with arrowroot and set aside.

In a saucepan, combine rhubarb and ¾ cup (150 g) sugar. Cover and cook over low heat for 5 minutes, until rhubarb releases its juices. Uncover and cook over medium heat, stirring frequently for 20 minutes, until most liquid evaporates and rhubarb has soft, jam-like consistency.

Combine rhubarb jam, soy creamer, remaining ¾ cup (175 ml) soymilk, and remaining ¾ cup (150 g) sugar in a saucepan and cook over low heat. Once mixture starts to boil, remove from heat and immediately add arrowroot cream. This will cause the liquid to thicken considerably.

Add vanilla extract.

Refrigerate mixture until chilled, approximately 2 to 3 hours. Freeze according to your ice cream maker's instructions.

Yield: 1 quart (approximately 600 g)

Tasty Tidbits

- Rhubarb is considered a vegetable, though it is most often treated as a fruit. It's rarely eaten raw.

- Rhubarb has been around for thousands of years, with records dating its use back to 2700 BC in China. There, it was cultivated for its medicinal properties (mainly as a diuretic).

SERVING SUGGESTION
Fresh Berry Coulis

"Coulis" is smooth sauce made from puréed fruits or vegetables, after they have been strained of their seeds and peels. This recipe can work with many combinations of berries.

⅓ pound (150 g) blueberries

⅓ pound (150 g) strawberries

⅓ pound (150 g) raspberries

1 cup (235 ml) plus 2 tablespoons (28 ml) organic white wine

2 tablespoons (42 g) agave nectar

2 bay leaves

¼ teaspoon ground allspice

1 teaspoon (5 ml) brandy

Purée berries, wine, and agave nectar in a blender. Pour into medium-size saucepan. Add bay leaves, allspice, and brandy.

Bring to simmer, stirring occasionally. Reduce heat, cover, and simmer 8 minutes.

Remove bay leaves and serve.

Yield: 4½ cups (1060 ml)

Papaya

This tropical ice cream flavor is great for a summer pick-me-up. One taste, and you'll know why Christopher Columbus exclaimed papya to be the "fruit of the angels."

1 cup (235 ml) soymilk, divided

2 tablespoons (16 g) arrowroot powder

2 papayas, seeded, peeled, and sliced

1 tablespoon (15 ml) freshly squeezed lemon juice

2 cups (470 ml) soy creamer

¾ cup (150 g) sugar

Pinch of salt

1 tablespoon (15 ml) vanilla extract

In a small bowl, combine ¼ cup (60 ml) soymilk with arrowroot and set aside.

In a food processor, blend papayas and lemon juice until smooth.

Combine blended papaya purée, soy creamer, remaining ¾ cup (175 ml) soymilk, sugar, and salt in a saucepan and cook over low heat. Once mixture begins to boil, remove from heat and immediately add arrowroot cream. This will cause the liquid to thicken noticeably.

Add vanilla extract.

Refrigerate mixture until chilled, approximately 2 to 3 hours. Freeze according to your ice cream maker's instructions.

Yield: 1 quart (approximately 600 g)

Tasty Tidbit

- The black seeds of the papaya are edible and can be ground up and used as a substitute for black pepper or added to salad dressing for a spicy kick.

SERVING SUGGESTION
Blackberry Consommé

"Consommé" is a clear, strong broth often served as the first course of a French meal. This recipe is perfect drizzled on Papaya ice cream and can be made with an assortment of berries or other fruit (mixed berry consommé is pictured).

2 quarts (1160 g) blackberries

1 cup (340 g) agave nectar

2 tablespoons (15 g) all-purpose flour

3 cups (710 ml) water

½ cup (115 g) vegan sour cream

½ cup (30 g) whipped soy topping (such as Soyatoo's soy whip)

½ cup (80 ml) blackberry brandy

Wash and clean blackberries. Place berries in a large pot of water (enough to cover the berries), bring to a boil, and simmer for 10 minutes over low heat. Drain berries and purée in blender. Set aside.

In a large bowl, combine agave nectar and flour. Stir in water, sour cream, whipped soy topping, and brandy. Pour mixture into a medium-size saucepan and cook over low heat. Add puréed berries. Slowly bring water to a boil, stirring constantly. Let boil for 2 minutes then let cool. Spoon over ice cream.

Yield: 3½ cups (825 ml)

Tasty Tidbits

- Apricots have a short season. Because of that, more than half of apricots grown are subsequently canned or dried.

- Greek mythology experts believe apricots are the "golden apples" of Hesperides—the fruit Hercules was ordered to pick in the 11th of his 12 labors.

Apricot

Apricots ripen earlier than other summer fruits. That means you can enjoy this tasty treat earlier in the season!

1 cup (235 ml) soymilk, divided

2 tablespoons (16 g) arrowroot powder

4 to 5 apricots, peeled and chopped, divided

2 cups (470 ml) soy creamer

¾ cup (150 g) sugar

1 tablespoon (15 ml) vanilla extract

1 tablespoon (15 ml) almond extract, optional

In a small bowl, combine ¼ cup (60 ml) soymilk and arrowroot and set aside.

Purée half of chopped apricots.

Combine puréed apricots, soy creamer, remaining ¾ cup (175 ml) soymilk, and sugar in a saucepan and cook over low heat. Once mixture starts to boil, remove from heat and immediately add arrowroot cream. This will cause the liquid to thicken noticeably.

Add vanilla extract. Add almond extract, if desired.

Refrigerate mixture until chilled, approximately 2 to 3 hours. Freeze according to your ice cream maker's instructions. In the last few minutes of freezing, stir in remaining chopped apricots.

Yield: 1 quart (approximately 600 g)

SERVING SUGGESTION

Fresh Balsamic Berries Tartare

"Tartare" is a thick white sauce typically made with mayonnaise, vinegar, and a variety of vegetables. This sweet version pairs exceptionally well with our Apricot ice cream for a refreshing flavor mix.

¾ cup (175 g) non-fat vegan mayonnaise or yogurt

¼ cup (35 g) blueberries

¼ cup (35 g) blackberries

2 tablespoons (28 ml) balsamic vinegar

Combine all ingredients in a small bowl and mix well. Serve promptly with ice cream.

Yield: 1¼ cups (approximately 185 g)

Green Apple

Always a favorite, this sour recipe tastes great with a sprinkle of brown sugar or cinnamon. Granny Smith apples work well for this classic.

1 cup (235 ml) soymilk, divided

2 tablespoons (16 g) arrowroot powder

3 medium-size green apples, peeled, cored, and sliced

2 tablespoons (28 ml) lemon juice

1 tablespoon (18 g) salt

2 cups (470 ml) soy creamer

¾ cup (150 g) sugar

1 tablespoon (15 ml) vanilla extract

In a small bowl, combine ¼ cup (60 ml) soymilk with arrowroot and set aside.

Peel, core, and slice apples. In a food processor, blend apples, lemon juice, and salt until smooth.

Combine apple mixture, soy creamer, remaining ¾ cup (175 ml) soymilk, and sugar in a medium-size saucepan and cook over low heat. Once mixture begins to boil, remove from heat and immediately add arrowroot cream. This will cause the liquid to thicken noticeably.

Add vanilla extract.

Refrigerate mixture until chilled, approximately 2 to 3 hours. Freeze according to your ice cream maker's instructions.

Yield: 1 quart (approximately 600 g)

Tasty Tidbits

- An apple packs more cancer-fighting antioxidant capability than a 1,500-milligram dose of vitamin C.

- Apples can rust. The flesh of an apple contains a chemical that reacts with oxygen just like metal. That's why it turns brown when exposed to the air.

- More than 7,000 varieties of apples are grown worldwide.

- Apples have five seed pockets, also known as carpel. The health and vigor of the plant determine the number of seeds contained in each carpel.

Green Fact

Animal agriculture contributes more to global warming than worldwide transportation emissions.

Watermelon Sorbet

Contrary to popular belief, watermelons are vegetables, part of the cucumber and squash family. No matter what you call them, the sweet, crisp flavor of this sorbet will win over anyone.

6 to 8 cups (900 to 1200 g) diced seedless watermelon

¼ cup (50 g) sugar

Zest of 1 lime, minced

Pinch of salt

½ cup (170 g) agave nectar

In a food processor, purée watermelon into 4 cups (940 ml) liquid.

In a large saucepan over medium heat, bring 1 cup (235 ml) watermelon purée, sugar, and lime peel to a simmer, stirring until sugar dissolves. Season with salt. Pour in remaining 3 cups (705 ml) watermelon purée, then add agave nectar, whisking until blended evenly.

Pour watermelon mixture into a metal cake pan and freeze overnight.

The next day, let frozen watermelon thaw at room temperature for 5 minutes. Using a knife, carefully break up purée into 2-inch (5-cm) pieces. Transfer to a food processor in batches and pulse until smooth.

Store sorbet in a freezer-safe container for up to one week.

Yield: 1 quart (approximately 600 g)

Tasty Tidbit

- Watermelons contain lycopene, an antioxidant thought to help reduce the risk of cancer and other diseases.

SERVING SUGGESTION

Salted Chocolate Pumpkin Seeds

This chocolate spin on a favorite autumn treat is a fantastic accompaniment to Watermelon sorbet.

2 cups (455 g) hulled pumpkin seeds (also known as pepitas)

1 tablespoon (15 ml) vegetable oil

1 teaspoon (6 g) salt

16 ounces (450 g) vegan chocolate

1 tablespoon (15 ml) soymilk, optional

Preheat oven to 350°F (180°C or gas mark 4).

Mix pumpkin seeds, oil, and salt in a bowl. Spread in a single layer on a cookie sheet. Bake for 10 to 15 minutes, stirring occasionally, until golden brown. Let cool, then place in a large bowl and set aside.

Cover another cookie sheet with waxed paper.

Place chocolate and soymilk (if using) in a double-boiler over low heat and stir frequently until melted. Pour half of chocolate over seeds, and mix until coated. Add more chocolate as needed to completely coat seeds. Turn seeds onto the cookie sheet, spreading them out into a single layer. Refrigerate until chocolate hardens and seeds can be broken apart from one another.

Yield: 2 cups (455 g) pumpkin seeds

Pear

Pears with brown speckles or "russets" on the skin are richer in flavor. Using these pears will yield great results every time.

1 cup (235 ml) soymilk, divided

2 tablespoons (16 g) arrowroot powder

2 to 3 ripe medium-size pears, thinly sliced

1 cup (235 ml) pear juice

1 tablespoon (15 ml) lemon juice

2 cups (470 ml) soy creamer

¾ cup (150 g) sugar

1 tablespoon (15 ml) vanilla extract

In a small bowl, combine ¼ cup (60 ml) soymilk with arrowroot and set aside.

Combine pears, pear juice, and lemon juice in heavy saucepan. Bring to boil over medium-high heat. Transfer to a food processor and purée until smooth. Chill for 10 to 15 minutes or until cold.

Combine pear-lemon mixture, soy creamer, remaining ¾ cup (175 ml) soymilk, and sugar in a saucepan and cook over low heat. Once mixture begins to boil, remove from heat and immediately add arrowroot cream. This will cause liquid to thicken noticeably.

Add vanilla extract.

Refrigerate mixture until chilled, approximately 2 to 3 hours. Freeze according to your ice cream maker's instructions.

Yield: 1 quart (approximately 600 g)

SERVING SUGGESTION

Sponge Cake

Our airy sponge cake paired with this sweet, subtle ice cream flavor is a winning combination.

Non-hydrogenated, non-dairy butter, for greasing

2 cups (250 g) self-rising flour

¼ cup (20 g) cocoa powder

1 tablespoon (14 g) baking powder

1⅓ cups (270 g) sugar

9 tablespoons (135 ml) vegetable oil

1 tablespoon (8 g) arrowroot powder

1½ cups (355 ml) water

Preheat oven to 325°F (170°C or gas mark 3). Grease two 8 x 8-inch (20 x 20-cm) shallow cake pans and line the base of each with greased waxed paper.

Sift flour, cocoa powder, and baking powder into a bowl. Add sugar, oil, arrowroot, and water. Mix well to a batter-like consistency. Pour mixture into prepared pans and bake for 40 minutes, until cakes spring back to a light touch in the center.

Turn cakes out onto wire rack and strip off waxed paper. Cool before serving.

Yield: 16 pieces

Tasty Tidbits

- There are more than 5,000 varieties of pears.

- Pear trees can produce fruit for up to 100 years.

Date

These sweet, sometimes honey-flavored fruits are great for flavoring ice cream. Plus, dates are high in dietary fiber. Who could ask for a better combination?

1 cup (235 ml) soymilk, divided

2 tablespoons (16 g) arrowroot powder

14 ounces (390 g) dried dates, pitted and chopped

2 cups (470 ml) soy creamer

¾ cup (150 g) sugar

1 tablespoon (15 ml) vanilla extract

In a small bowl, combine ¼ cup (60 ml) soymilk with arrowroot and set aside.

In a food processor, purée dates until smooth.

Combine date mixture, soy creamer, remaining ¾ cup (175 ml) soymilk, and sugar in a saucepan and cook over low heat. Once mixture begins to boil, remove from heat and immediately add arrowroot cream. This will cause the liquid to thicken noticeably.

Add vanilla extract.

Refrigerate mixture until chilled, approximately 2 to 3 hours. Freeze according to your ice cream maker's instructions.

Yield: 1 quart (approximately 600 g)

Green Fact

By eating vegan for a month, you free up the quarter-acre (1012 sq m) of land (which is normally required to feed a meat-eating person).

CHAPTER 3

Healthy Flavors

Working for Mr. De Leon became a challenging job because I had to come up with fresh and flavorful ideas. How do you satisfy someone obsessed with dairy and meat, but who shouldn't eat it?

After mastering the basic ice cream recipe, the pressure was on to prove to people that I could create low-calorie, low-sugar desserts that still tasted good. This is when I switched from making regular ice cream to vegan ice cream.

In my quest for the finest ingredients, I realized that when I used animal-free products, I automatically cut calories and increased health benefits— without even trying! By adding healthy mix-ins such as açai berries or flaxseed, the nutritional value of the ice cream skyrocketed.

Good thing I've never backed down from a challenge.

Lavender Mint

Health Benefit: Cleansing

Refreshing mint, paired with natural, cleansing lavender clears the mind and rejuvenates the body. Garnish with mint sprigs and enjoy.

1 cup (235 ml) soymilk, divided

2 tablespoons (16 g) arrowroot powder

1 cup (40 g) lavender leaves and flowers

2 cups (470 ml) soy creamer

¾ cup (150 g) sugar

1 tablespoon (15 ml) peppermint extract

1 tablespoon (15 ml) vanilla extract

In a small bowl, combine ¼ cup (60 ml) soymilk with arrowroot and set aside.

In a food processor, blend ½ cup (120 ml) soymilk with lavender leaves and flowers (reserving a handful of flowers for later) until smooth. Set aside.

Mix soy creamer, remaining ¼ cup (60 ml) soymilk, and sugar in a saucepan and cook over low heat. Once mixture begins to boil, remove from heat and immediately add arrowroot cream. This will cause the liquid to thicken noticeably. Add peppermint and vanilla extracts.

Refrigerate mixture until chilled, approximately 2 to 3 hours. Add blended lavender milk and freeze according to your ice cream maker's instructions. In the last few minutes of churning, sprinkle any leftover lavender flowers (stripped from the lower heads) into ice cream.

Yield: 1 quart (approximately 600 g)

Tasty Tidbits

- The word "lavender" comes from the Latin word *lavare* meaning "to wash." In ancient Rome, lavender was used as a ritual bathing herb.

- In Medieval times, lavender was used as protection. A lavender cross hung over a door safeguarded against disease and warded off evil.

Tasty Tidbit

- Capsaicin is the compound found in peppers that is responsible for causing an increase in one's metabolic rate after consumption. This increase results in more calories burned—and a happier you!

Vanilla Chile Pepper

Health Benefit: Metabolism Boost

A kicked-up flavor for spice lovers, this ice cream is anything but "vanilla." Try serving it on a sugar cone (page 200) to balance out the spice.

3 medium-size chile peppers (cayenne or jalapeño peppers work well)

1 cup (235 ml) soymilk, divided

2 tablespoons (16 g) arrowroot powder

2 cups (470 ml) soy creamer

½ cup (100 g) sugar

1 tablespoon (15 ml) vanilla extract

In a blender, process chile peppers until smooth. Set aside.

In a small bowl, combine ¼ cup (60 ml) soymilk with arrowroot and set aside.

Mix soy creamer, remaining ¾ cup (175 ml) soymilk, and sugar in a saucepan and cook over low heat. Once mixture begins to boil, remove from heat and immediately add arrowroot cream. This will cause the liquid to thicken noticeably. Add vanilla extract.

Refrigerate mixture until chilled, approximately 2 to 3 hours. Freeze according to your ice cream maker's instructions. In the last few minutes of churning, add blended chile peppers.

Yield: 1 quart (approximately 600 g)

Green Fact

Well-planned vegan and vegetarian diets work during any stage of life, including pregnancy, lactation, infancy, childhood, and adolescence.

Vanilla Hazelnut

Health Benefit: Energy Boost

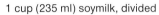

Hazelnuts are packed with protein and antioxidants and give this ice cream a lovely crunch and flavor.

1 cup (235 ml) soymilk, divided

2 tablespoons (16 g) arrowroot powder

2 cups (470 ml) soy creamer

½ cup (100 g) sugar

1 tablespoon (15 ml) vanilla extract

1 tablespoon (15 ml) hazelnut extract

¾ cup (85 g) chopped roasted hazelnuts

In a small bowl, combine ¼ cup (60 ml) soymilk with arrowroot and set aside.

Mix soy creamer, remaining ¾ cup (175 ml) soymilk, and sugar in a saucepan and cook over low heat. Once mixture begins to boil, remove from heat and immediately add arrowroot cream. This will cause the liquid to thicken noticeably.

Add vanilla and hazelnut extracts.

Refrigerate mixture until chilled, approximately 2 to 3 hours. Freeze according to your ice cream maker's instructions. In the last few minutes of churning, add chopped hazelnuts.

Yield: 1 quart (approximately 600 g)

Tasty Tidbit

- Hazelnut trees bloom and pollinate in the middle of winter. Wind carries the pollen to a tiny red flower on the tree, where it stays dormant until June, when the nut begins to form.

SERVING SUGGESTION

Roasted Agave Apricots

Fresh apricots drenched in agave syrup and roasted in brown sugar pair wonderfully with our delicious Vanilla Hazelnut ice cream.

12 small or medium fresh apricots, halved and pitted

3 tablespoons (64 g) agave nectar

2 tablespoons (28 g) non-hydrogenated, non-dairy butter

2 tablespoons (20 g) brown sugar

Preheat oven to 375°F (190°C or gas mark 5).

Arrange apricots cut-side up in a 10-inch (25-cm) skillet so they are close together. Drizzle agave nectar over apricots. Put a small piece of butter into each apricot cavity. Sprinkle brown sugar over the top and place in oven. Roast for 15 minutes.

After the 15 minutes are up, raise temperature to 400°F (200°C or gas mark 6). From that point on, baste apricots with pan juices every 10 minutes until apricots begin to caramelize and liquid reduces to a saucy consistency, about 45 minutes total (including the initial 15-minute roasting time).

Yield: 24 apricot halves

Vanilla Cardamom

Health Benefit: Aromatherapy

*Serve this ice cream with a vegan muffin **(as pictured)** and you'll be in heaven.*

1 cup (235 ml) soymilk, divided

2 tablespoons (16 g) arrowroot powder

2 cups (470 ml) soy creamer

¾ cup (150 g) sugar

1 tablespoon (15 ml) vanilla extract

⅛ teaspoon cardamom

In a small bowl, combine ¼ cup (60 ml) soymilk with arrowroot and set aside.

Mix soy creamer, remaining ¾ cup (175 ml) soymilk, and sugar in a saucepan and cook over low heat. Once mixture begins to boil, remove from heat and immediately add arrowroot cream. This will cause the liquid to thicken noticeably. Add vanilla extract.

Refrigerate mixture until chilled, approximately 2 to 3 hours. Mix in cardamom. Freeze according to your ice cream maker's instructions.

Yield: 1 quart (approximately 600 g)

Ginger Ginseng

Health Benefit: Restoration

A natural remedy for nausea, flu, and poor circulation meets ice cream.

3½ cups (825 ml) coconut milk, divided

2 tablespoons (16 g) arrowroot powder

½ cup (48 g) minced ginger

¾ cup (150 g) sugar

1 tablespoon (15 ml) vanilla extract

1 tablespoon (15 ml) ginseng extract

1 tablespoon (15 ml) coconut extract

¾ cup (170 g) crystallized ginger pieces

In a small bowl, combine ¼ cup (60 ml) coconut milk with arrowroot and set aside.

Mix remaining 3¼ cups (765 ml) coconut milk and minced ginger in a medium-size saucepan and bring to a boil over low heat. Remove from heat and set aside to steep for 25 minutes. Strain through a fine-mesh sieve to remove minced ginger. .

Combine ginger-coconut milk and sugar and cook over low heat. Once mixture begins to boil, remove from heat and immediately add arrowroot cream. Add extracts.

Refrigerate mixture until chilled, approximately 2 to 3 hours. Freeze according to your ice cream maker's instructions. In the last few minutes of churning, add crystallized ginger.

Yield: 1 quart (approximately 600 g)

Cinnamon Ginkgo

Health Benefit: Focus and Memory

This rich, creamy cinnamon-ginkgo blend improves the memory and promotes general longevity. Plus, it tastes delicious!

1 cup (235 ml) soymilk, divided

2 tablespoons (16 g) arrowroot powder

2 cups (470 ml) soy creamer

2 teaspoons (5 g) ground cinnamon

¾ cup (150 g) sugar

1 tablespoon (15 ml) vanilla extract

¾ cup (110 g) ginkgo nuts, roasted and chopped

In a small bowl, combine ¼ cup (60 ml) soymilk with arrowroot and set aside.

Mix soy creamer, remaining ¾ cup (175 ml) soymilk, cinnamon, and sugar in a saucepan and cook over low heat. Once mixture begins to boil, remove from heat and immediately add arrowroot cream. This will cause the liquid to thicken noticeably. Add vanilla extract.

Refrigerate mixture until chilled, approximately 2 to 3 hours. Freeze according to your ice cream maker's instructions. In the last few minutes of churning, add chopped ginkgo nuts.

Yield: 1 quart (approximately 600 g)

Tasty Tidbits

- Ginkgo nuts are widely used in Asian cooking and are similar in texture to soybeans. Look for them in Asian markets.

- An extract of *Ginkgo biloba* can be found in tablet or liquid form and is used to improve memory.

SERVING SUGGESTION

Blackberry Confit

A "fruit confit" is a jam-like substance made by preserving fresh fruit in sugar. This blackberry version is a delightful accompaniment to our Cinnamon Ginkgo ice cream.

1 cup (200 g) sugar

1 cup (235 ml) water

1 tablespoon (15 ml) vanilla extract

½ cup (170 g) agave nectar

2 cups (290 g) blackberries

Fresh peppermint leaves, chopped

In small saucepan, combine sugar, water, vanilla extract, and agave nectar. Bring to a boil and reduce heat to medium. Simmer 3 to 4 minutes.

Place blackberries into a medium-size bowl. Pour sauce directly over blackberries and add chopped peppermint.

Serve over ice cream or place in jars to refrigerate.

Yield: 3½ cups (1120 ml)

Avocado Lemon

This flavor combination, common in salad recipes, offers a unique, smooth taste and amazing health benefits.

3 ripe avocados

3 tablespoons (45 ml) lemon juice

½ cup (100 g) sugar

2 cups (470 ml) soy creamer

1 cup (235 ml) soymilk

1 tablespoon (15 ml) vanilla extract

¼ cup (24 g) lemon zest

Peel avocados, then place flesh in a blender. Add lemon juice, sugar, and soy creamer and purée until smooth. Pour mixture into a large bowl and whisk in soymilk. Add vanilla extract and lemon zest.

Pour into ice cream maker and freeze according to instructions.

Yield: 1 quart (approximately 600 g)

Pomegranate Grapefruit

Pomegranates and grapefruits both greatly reduce the risk of heart disease by lowering cholesterol and preventing blood clots. This powerful combination of fruit blended into one ice cream is sure to impress.

1 cup (235 ml) soymilk, divided

2 tablespoons (16 g) arrowroot powder

1 cup (235 ml) pomegranate juice

2 tablespoons (12 g) grapefruit zest

1 cup (235 ml) grapefruit juice

2 cups (470 ml) soy creamer

¾ cup (150 g) sugar

1 tablespoon (15 ml) vanilla extract

In a small bowl, combine ¼ cup (60 ml) soymilk with arrowroot and set aside.

Combine pomegranate juice, zest, grapefruit juice, soy creamer, remaining ¾ cup (175 ml) soymilk, and sugar in a saucepan and cook over low heat. Once mixture begins to boil, remove from heat and immediately add arrowroot cream. This will cause the liquid to thicken noticeably. Add vanilla extract.

Refrigerate mixture until chilled, approximately 2 to 3 hours. Freeze according to your ice cream maker's instructions.

Yield: 1 quart (approximately 600 g)

Sweet Potato Basil

Health Benefit: Stress Relief

Starchy "comfort" foods like sweet potatoes calm us down because they raise the levels of mood-enhancing serotonin in our bodies. Throw in some basil and poof: a flavor that's easy to love—and unlike any other.

4 to 5 medium-size sweet potatoes

1½ cups (300 g) sugar, divided

2 to 3 teaspoons (4.5 to 7 g) nutmeg

1 cup (235 ml) soymilk, divided

2 tablespoons (16 g) arrowroot powder

3 tablespoons (8 g) packed fresh basil

2 cups (470 ml) soy creamer

Dash of salt

1 tablespoon (15 ml) vanilla extract

Bake sweet potatoes at 400°F (200°C or gas mark 6) for 40 to 50 minutes. Mash and stir in ¾ cup (150 g) sugar and nutmeg. Cool.

In a small bowl, combine ¼ cup (60 ml) soymilk with arrowroot and set aside.

Combine ¼ cup (60 ml) soymilk and basil in food processor and blend until basil is very finely ground. Set aside.

Mix soy creamer, remaining ½ cup (120 ml) soymilk, remaining ¾ cup (150 g) sugar, and salt in a saucepan and cook over low heat. Once mixture begins to boil, remove from heat and immediately add arrowroot cream. This will cause the liquid to thicken noticeably.

Add vanilla extract.

Refrigerate mixture until chilled, approximately 2 to 3 hours. Add sweet potato mixture and blended basil and freeze according to your ice cream maker's instructions.

Yield: 1 quart (approximately 600 g)

Dark Chocolate Açai Berry

Health Benefit: Antioxidant Boost

Native to Central and South America, the açai berry is the hottest new super-fruit to hit the produce scene. Most commonly available in pulp or juice form, açai contains powerful antioxidants that boost the immune system and fight disease. Paired with dark chocolate, this ice cream does a body good!

1 cup (235 ml) soymilk, divided

2 tablespoons (16 g) arrowroot powder

2 cups (470 ml) soy creamer

¾ cup (150 g) sugar

¼ cup (20 g) cocoa powder

½ cup (90 g) vegan dark chocolate chips

¾ cup (195 g) açai pulp or purée

1 tablespoon (15 ml) vanilla extract

In a small bowl, combine ¼ cup (60 ml) soymilk with arrowroot and set aside.

Mix soy creamer, remaining ¾ cup (175 ml) soymilk, sugar, cocoa powder, and chocolate chips in a saucepan over low heat. Stir until the chocolate chips are melted. Add the açai pulp, then bring the mixture to a boil. Once it starts to boil, remove from heat and immediately add arrowroot cream. This will cause the liquid to thicken noticeably.

Add vanilla extract.

Refrigerate mixture until chilled, approximately 2 to 3 hours. Freeze according to your ice cream maker's instructions. In the last few minutes of churning, add in açai berries.

Yield: 1 quart (approximately 600 g)

Tasty Tidbits

- The juice of the açai berry is said to taste like a combination of blueberries and chocolate.

- The juice of the açai berry is being tested for its use as a dyeing agent in the preparation of patients undergoing MRI scans of the gastrointestinal tract.

Green Fact

Diets high in fruits and vegetables are associated with a reduced risk of cardiovascular disease, cancer, and chronic diseases such as diabetes and asthma.

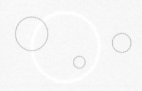

Peanut Butter Flaxseed

Health Benefit: Protein Power

If you like nuts, this is the ice cream for you. Both main ingredients offer different but complementary nutty flavors. Try adding this to a breakfast shake for a protein-filled start to your day.

1 cup (170 g) flaxseed

1 cup (240 ml) soymilk

2 cups (470 ml) soy creamer

¾ cup (195 g) peanut butter

½ cup (75 g) brown sugar

1 tablespoon (15 ml) vanilla extract

In a blender, grind flaxseed. Set aside.

In a medium-size saucepan over medium heat, combine soymilk, soy creamer, peanut butter, flaxseed, and brown sugar. Cook over low heat. Once mixture starts to boil, remove from heat.

Add vanilla extract.

Refrigerate mixture until chilled, approximately 2 to 3 hours. Freeze according to your ice cream maker's instructions. Sprinkle with whole flaxseeds when serving, if desired.

Yield: 1 quart (approximately 600 g)

Tasty Tidbits

- Flax is an ancient crop that was used as a food source as far back as 3000 BC.

- Flaxseed is a powerful source of omega-3 fatty acids, which have been shown to improve brain function, and according to the U.S. Food and Drug Administration, reduce the risk of coronary heart disease.

SERVING SUGGESTION

Crunchy Peanut Butter Sauce

For even more peanut-buttery goodness, drizzle this crunchy sauce over your scoop.

1 cup (260 g) chunky peanut butter

¼ cup (60 ml) soymilk

¼ cup (60 g) agave nectar

¼ teaspoon cinnamon

¼ cup (35 g) chopped peanuts

Warm peanut butter, soymilk, and agave nectar in a small skillet over low heat. Stir until smooth.

Sprinkle with cinnamon, stirring until combined, then add peanuts. Serve while still warm.

Yield: 2 cups (470 ml)

Tasty Tidbits

- Berries, like citrus fruit, will not ripen once picked.

- Blackberries and are easily mistaken for the similar-looking black raspberries. Here's a simple way to tell them apart: The name "black raspberry" is two words with a space in between—much like the hollow center of a black raspberry. "Blackberry" is one word and does not have a hollow center.

- The blackberry is an aggregate fruit composed of many smaller fruits called "drupes."

Blackberry and Oats

Health Benefit: Antioxidant Boost

We've all heard that oats can help lower your cholesterol, but did you also know that they are a rich source of selenium, an antioxidant and micro-mineral that helps protect your cells from free-radical damage? To boot, blackberries are particularly high in anthocyanins, another powerful class of antioxidants that can help reduce inflammation. The two pair wonderfully together in this rich, creamy, and delightfully purple ice cream.

½ cup (40 g) oats

¼ cup (60 ml) almond milk

1 cup (235 ml) soymilk, divided

2 tablespoons (16 g) arrowroot powder

1 cup (145 g) blackberries

2 cups (470 ml) soy creamer

¾ cup (150 g) sugar

1 tablespoon (15 ml) vanilla extract

1 tablespoon (15 ml) almond extract

In a food processor, blend oats and almond milk until smooth. Cover and set aside.

In a small bowl, combine ¼ cup (60 ml) soymilk with arrowroot and set aside.

Purée blackberries, soy creamer, remaining ¾ cup (175 ml) soymilk, and sugar in a blender. Pour mixture into a saucepan and cook over low heat. Once mixture begins to boil, remove from heat and immediately add arrowroot cream. This will cause the liquid to thicken noticeably.

Add vanilla and almond extracts.

Refrigerate mixture until chilled, approximately 2 to 3 hours. Add oat-almond milk mixture and freeze according to your ice cream maker's instructions.

Yield: 1 quart (approximately 600 g)

Sweet Curry Coconut

Health Benefit: Essential Oils

Coconut, whose oil is highly regarded for its levels of the essential fatty acid lauric acid, is a flavorful companion to the sweet curry spice in this recipe. You'll get swept away by the taste.

3½ cups (825 ml) coconut milk, divided

2 tablespoons (16 g) arrowroot powder

¾ cup (150 g) sugar

1 tablespoon (15 ml) vanilla extract

1 tablespoon (15 ml) coconut extract

½ cup (50 g) curry spice

¾ cup (60 g) shredded coconut

In a small bowl, combine ¼ cup (60 ml) coconut milk with arrowroot and set aside.

Mix remaining 3¼ cups (765 ml) coconut milk and sugar in a saucepan, and cook over low heat. Once mixture begins to boil, remove from heat and immediately add arrowroot cream. This will cause the liquid to thicken noticeably.

Stir in vanilla and coconut extracts.

Refrigerate mixture until chilled, approximately 2 to 3 hours. Mix curry spice into ice cream and freeze according to your ice cream maker's instructions. In the last few minutes of churning, add shredded coconut.

Yield: 1 quart (approximately 600 g)

Tasty Tidbit

- The word "curry" derived from the Tamil word *kari*, meaning "spiced sauce."

SERVING SUGGESTION

Grilled Figs with Rosemary and Agave

This delicious creation is perfect for a backyard grill. Serve over ice cream or as a snack.

6 fresh figs, trimmed and halved

2 tablespoons (42 g) agave nectar

2 tablespoons (3 g) chopped fresh rosemary

Grill figs over medium-high heat for 6 to 8 minutes, turning once halfway through.

Divide between two plates. Drizzle agave nectar over each plate, then top with chopped rosemary.

Yield: 12 halves or 4 servings

Carob Apricot

Health Benefit: Fiber Boost

Searching for a healthier alternative to chocolate that doesn't sacrifice taste? Look no further than carob. This treat is naturally caffeine-free, low in fat and sodium, and high in fiber. Paired with apricots, it creates a smooth, tangy ice cream.

1 cup (235 ml) soymilk, divided

2 tablespoons (16 g) arrowroot

2 cups (470 ml) soy creamer

¾ cup (150 g) sugar

¾ cup (75 g) carob powder

1 tablespoon (15 ml) vanilla extract

½ cup (85 g) apricots, peeled and chopped

In a small bowl, combine ¼ cup (60 ml) soymilk with arrowroot and set aside.

Mix soy creamer, remaining ¾ cup (175 ml) soymilk, sugar, and carob powder in a saucepan and cook over low heat. Once mixture begins to boil, remove from heat and immediately add arrowroot cream. This will cause the liquid to thicken noticeably. Add vanilla extract.

Refrigerate mixture until chilled, approximately 2 to 3 hours. Freeze according to your ice cream maker's instructions. In the last few minutes of churning, add apricot pieces.

Yield: 1 quart (approximately 600 g)

Green Fact

Vegan and vegetarian diets significantly lower saturated fat and cholesterol in the body.

Raspberry Dandelion

Health Benefit: Vitamin A

Dandelions are not just pesky weeds in your garden—they are nature's richest green-vegetable source of beta carotene, from which vitamin A is created. How's that for a reason to give this pink, aromatic flavor a try?

1 cup (235 ml) soymilk, divided

1 cup (40 g) dandelion leaves and flowers

2 tablespoons (16 g) arrowroot powder

1 cup (125 g) raspberries

2 cups (470 ml) soy creamer

¾ cup (150 g) sugar

1 tablespoon (15 ml) vanilla extract

In a food processor, blend ¾ cup (175 ml) soymilk with dandelion leaves and flowers until smooth.

In a small bowl, combine remaining ¼ cup (60 ml) soymilk with arrowroot and set aside.

Purée raspberries, dandelion mixture, soy creamer, and sugar in a blender until smooth. Pour mixture into a saucepan and cook over low heat. Once mixture begins to boil, remove from heat and immediately add arrowroot cream. This will cause the liquid to thicken noticeably.

Add vanilla extract.

Refrigerate mixture until chilled, approximately 2 to 3 hours. Freeze according to your ice cream maker's instructions.

Yield: 1 quart (approximately 600 g)

Tasty Tidbits

- The word "dandelion" comes from the French *dent de lion* or "tooth of the lion," which refers to the jagged edges of the plant's leaf.

- The flowers of dandelions close at night.

Green Fact

Following a balanced, plant-based diet will provide adequate amounts of all the essential amino acids you need.

Oats and Fig

Health Benefit: Magnesium and Potassium Boost

Oats are rich in magnesium, which lowers the risk of type 2 diabetes and aids in the prevention of breast cancer. Figs are a great source of dietary fiber, and also contain potassium, which helps control blood pressure. The two work deliciously together in this rich, heady treat.

½ cup (40 g) oats

1¼ cup (295 ml) almond milk, divided

2 tablespoons (16 g) arrowroot powder

20 fresh figs, chopped

½ cup (120 ml) water

1 cup (200 g) sugar, divided

2 cups (470 ml) soy creamer

Pinch of salt

1 teaspoon (5 ml) lemon juice

1 tablespoon (15 ml) vanilla extract

1 tablespoon (15 ml) almond extract

In a food processor, blend oats and ¼ cup (60 ml) almond milk until smooth. Set aside.

In a small bowl, combine ¼ cup (60 ml) almond milk with arrowroot and set aside.

Remove stems from figs and chop the fruit into small pieces. Place figs in a saucepan with water and ¼ cup (50 g) sugar. Cook mixture over medium heat, stirring occasionally, until it becomes thick, soft, and jam-like.

Combine fig mixture, soy creamer, remaining ¾ cup (175 ml) almond milk, and remaining ¾ cup (150 g) sugar in a saucepan and cook over low heat. Add salt and lemon juice. Once mixture begins to boil, remove from heat and immediately add arrowroot cream. This will cause the liquid to thicken noticeably.

Add vanilla and almond extracts and oat mixture.

Refrigerate mixture until chilled, approximately 2 to 3 hours. Freeze according to your ice cream maker's instructions.

Yield: 1 quart (approximately 600 g)

Tasty Tidbits

- Figs provide more fiber, in both soluble and insoluble forms, than any other common fruit or vegetable.

- Although it's typically regarded as a fruit, the fig is actually a flower that is inverted into itself. The seeds, or drupes, are the real fruit.

Orange Dragon Fruit

Health Benefit: Immune Boost

This colorful, antioxidant-rich ice cream boosts the immune system while regulating cholesterol levels and destroying free radicals. Plus, with an ingredient called "dragon fruit," who wouldn't want to try it?

1 cup (235 ml) soymilk, divided

2 tablespoons (16 g) arrowroot powder

2 large navel oranges

2 dragon fruits

2 cups (470 ml) soy creamer

¾ cup (150 g) sugar

1 tablespoon (15 ml) vanilla extract

In a small bowl, combine ¼ cup (60 ml) soymilk with arrowroot and set aside.

Finely grate 2 tablespoons (12 g) zest from oranges, then halve oranges and squeeze 1 cup (235 ml) juice. Discard oranges.

Remove dragon fruit flesh from skin, add to blender, and process until smooth.

Combine zest, orange juice, dragon fruit purée, soy creamer, remaining ¾ cup (175 ml) soymilk, and sugar in a saucepan and cook over low heat. Once mixture begins to boil, remove from heat and immediately add arrowroot cream. This will cause the liquid to thicken noticeably.

Add vanilla extract.

Refrigerate mixture until chilled, approximately 2 to 3 hours. Freeze according to your ice cream maker's instructions.

Yield: 1 quart (approximately 600 g)

Tasty Tidbits

- The dragon fruit has many names: Red Pitahaya or Red Pitaya, Night Blooming Cereus, Strawberry Pear, Belle of the Night.

- Dragon fruit is known to reduce blood glucose levels and may therefore be helpful in the control of type 2 diabetes.

Green Fact

Organic, locally grown food is great for your body and the environment. Eating one meal per week comprised of locally grown food could reduce oil consumption significantly.

Spicy Chocolate Twist

Health Benefit: Healing Power

A spectacular variation on classic chocolate ice cream, this recipe is great for those who want a rich and spicy flavor.

1 cup (235 ml) soymilk, divided

2 tablespoons (16 g) arrowroot powder

2 cups (470 ml) soy creamer

¾ cup (150 g) sugar

¼ cup (20 g) cocoa powder

½ cup (90 g) vegan Mexican chocolate disks (or substitute ½ cup [90 g] vegan chocolate chips and ¼ cup [28 g] cinnamon)

1 tablespoon (15 ml) vanilla extract

2 tablespoons (10 g) cayenne pepper, or to taste

In a small bowl, combine ¼ cup (60 ml) soymilk with arrowroot and set aside.

Pour soy creamer, remaining ¾ cup (175 ml) soymilk, sugar, cocoa powder, and chocolate into a medium-size saucepan. Stirring frequently on low heat, melt chocolate, then bring mixture to a boil. Once it begins to boil, remove from heat and immediately add arrowroot cream. This will cause the liquid to thicken noticeably.

Add vanilla extract.

Refrigerate mixture until chilled, approximately 2 to 3 hours. Mix in cayenne pepper. Freeze according to your ice cream maker's instructions.

Yield: 1 quart (approximately 600 g)

> ✳Variation: Spicy Chocolate Chocolate Chip
> If you like lots of bits and pieces in your ice cream, add ½ cup (90 g) of vegan chocolate chips during the last few minutes of churning. Nuts would also work well—just use the same amount.

Tasty Tidbits

• Cayenne pepper increases circulation and stimulates heart muscles. In fact, just one teaspoon (1.8 g) of this spice has been known to revive heart-attack victims from an unconscious state.

• Mexican chocolate is dark, bitter chocolate mixed with sugar, cinnamon, and occasionally, nuts.

CHAPTER 4

Asian Flavors

"Sweet, sour, bitter, pungent. All must be tasted."

—Chinese Proverb

Asia is the world's largest and most geographically diverse continent. Those characteristics make it subject to the world's widest climatic extremes, and consequently, the most varied forms of vegetation on earth.

I spend at least a few days each month visiting Asian countries, sampling thousands of fruits, vegetables, spices, and teas to use in new, exotic ice cream flavors.

A five-day hike through the tropical forests of southwestern China inspired our refreshing eucalyptus flavor. An exciting night at a *sushi-ya* (a sushi bar) in Tokyo prompted the spicy wasabi ice cream.

Take your own trip around the continent by sampling these spicy and savory Asian-inspired delicacies. Your palate won't be disappointed.

Yam

This bright-colored ice cream has a delicious, incomparable flavor. Topped with crispy nuts, it's a welcome addition to any autumn or winter menu.

4 to 5 yams

2 to 3 teaspoons (4 to 7 g) ground nutmeg

Dash of salt

1 cup (235 ml) soymilk, divided

2 tablespoons (16 g) arrowroot powder

2 cups (470 ml) soy creamer

¾ cu p (150 g) sugar

1 tablespoon (15 ml) vanilla extract

Bake yams at 400°F (200°C or gas mark 6) for 40 to 50 minutes. Cool slightly and remove skins. Mash and add nutmeg and salt. Let cool.

In a small bowl, combine ¼ cup (60 ml) soymilk with arrowroot and set aside.

Mix soy creamer, remaining ¾ cup (175 ml) soymilk, and sugar in a saucepan and cook over low heat. Once mixture begins to boil, remove from heat and immediately add arrowroot cream. This will cause the liquid to thicken noticeably.

Add vanilla extract.

Refrigerate mixture until chilled, approximately 2 to 3 hours. Add mashed yams. Freeze according to your ice cream maker's instructions.

Yield: 1 quart (approximately 600 g)

Tasty Tidbits

- Sweet potatoes are often mistakenly called yams, but the two are different vegetables. Yams contain more natural sugar than sweet potatoes and have a higher moisture content. Look for them at Latin American and Caribbean markets.

- The Southeast Asian water yam grows up to 8-feet (2.4-m) long and can weigh more than 100 pounds (45 kg).

- Six hundred species of yam exist, but only 150 are cultivated for food.

SERVING SUGGESTION

Crispy Caramelized Hazelnuts

When hazelnuts caramelize, their natural sugars darken to a golden brown and a rich, delicious flavor develops.

10 to 12 large hazelnuts

¼ cup (85 g) agave nectar

½ cup (120 ml) water

Place each nut on a wooden or metal skewer.

In a small saucepan over medium heat, mix agave nectar and water. Cover and heat. Do not stir. Continue cooking without stirring until syrup turns a medium-dark amber color, 4 to 5 minutes.

Remove from heat and quickly dip each skewered nut into syrup. Prop skewers over waxed paper so nuts can drip and harden. Once cool, remove nuts from skewers and sprinkle over ice cream.

Yield: 10 to 12 hazelnuts

Sweet Cucumber

The inner temperature of a cucumber can be 20 degrees cooler than the outside air. That makes it a perfect ingredient for ice cream!

Tasty Tidbits

- Cucumbers belong to the same family as pumpkins, zucchini, watermelon, and other squash.

- The flesh of a cucumber is primarily composed of water, but also contains vitamin C, which helps soothe skin irritations and reduces swelling.

1 cup (235 ml) soymilk, divided

2 tablespoons (16 g) arrowroot powder

1 large cucumber

¾ cup (150 g) plus 2 tablespoons (25 g) sugar, divided

1 cup (235 ml) water

Juice from 2 lemons

2 cups (470 ml) soy creamer

1 tablespoon (15 ml) vanilla extract

In a small bowl, combine ¼ cup (60 ml) soymilk with arrowroot and set aside.

Peel cucumber, remove seeds, and cut into pieces. In a saucepan, combine cucumber pieces, 2 tablespoons (25 g) sugar, and water. Cook over medium heat until tender.

In a food processor, blend cooked cucumbers and lemon juice until smooth.

Mix soy creamer, remaining ¾ cup (175 ml) soymilk, remaining ¾ cup (150 g) sugar, and blended cucumber in a saucepan and cook over low heat. Once mixture begins to boil, remove from heat and immediately add arrowroot cream. This will cause the liquid to thicken noticeably.

Add vanilla extract.

Refrigerate mixture until chilled, approximately 2 to 3 hours. Freeze according to your ice cream maker's instructions.

Yield: 1 quart (approximately 600 g)

SERVING SUGGESTION
Fruit Tempura

Tempura is a Japanese specialty, prepared by dipping fruit or vegetables into batter and deep-frying until crispy. For this recipe, use any fruit you like. Note: Larger slices work best.

1 cup (125 g) all-purpose flour

½ teaspoon salt

¼ teaspoon agave nectar

1 teaspoon (4.6 g) baking powder

1 cup (235 ml) water

½ cup (120 ml) vegetable oil, divided

Mixed fruit (bananas, peaches, apricots, apples, and pineapples)

Combine flour, salt, agave nectar, and baking powder in a medium-size bowl. Slowly add water and 3 tablespoons (45 ml) oil and stir until smooth and creamy. Chill for 15 minutes.

Heat several inches of vegetable oil in a wok or large frying pan over high heat. Dip fruit into batter, then carefully drop into oil. Allow to fry for 3 minutes, until crisp and lightly golden brown. Drain on a paper towel.

Yield: 2 cups (approximately 250 g)

Black Sesame

Open sesame! This ice cream gets its nutty, delicately sweet flavor from the seeds, which are used in many Chinese teas and soups.

1 cup (235 ml) soymilk, divided

2 tablespoons (16 g) arrowroot powder

2 cups (470 ml) soy creamer

3 tablespoons (24 g) black sesame seeds, crushed

½ cup (100 g) sugar

1 tablespoon (15 ml) vanilla extract

In a small bowl, combine ¼ cup (60 ml) soymilk with arrowroot and set aside.

Mix soy creamer, remaining ¾ cup (175 ml) soymilk, sesame seeds, and sugar in a saucepan and cook over low heat. Once mixture begins to boil, remove from heat and immediately add arrowroot cream. This will cause the liquid to thicken noticeably.

Add vanilla extract.

Refrigerate mixture until chilled, approximately 2 to 3 hours. Freeze according to your ice cream maker's instructions.

Yield: 1 quart (approximately 600 g)

Tasty Tidbit

• The famous phrase "open sesame" can be attributed to the fact that ripe sesame seeds burst from their pods with a sharp popping noise.

Green Fact

Current research links contaminated dairy products to Crohn's disease, a disorder that causes inflammation of the gastrointestinal tract. Seventy-five percent of patients with Crohn's disease tested positive for a certain bacteria found in dairy cows.

Wasabi

Wasabi root has a fruity fragrance with a spiciness that packs a punch, but doesn't linger. Give your sinuses—and your palate—a treat with this stimulating ice cream flavor.

1 cup (235 ml) soymilk

2 tablespoons (16 g) arrowroot powder

2 cups (470 ml) soy creamer

1 tablespoon (10 g) wasabi paste

¾ cup (150 g) sugar

1 tablespoon (15 ml) vanilla extract

In a small bowl, combine ¼ cup (60 ml) soymilk with arrowroot and set aside.

Mix soy creamer, remaining ¾ cup (175 ml) soymilk, wasabi paste, and sugar in a saucepan and cook over low heat. Once mixture begins to boil, remove from heat and immediately add arrowroot cream. This will cause the liquid to thicken noticeably.

Add vanilla extract.

Refrigerate mixture until chilled, approximately 2 to 3 hours. Freeze according to your ice cream maker's instructions.

Yield: 1 quart (approximately 600 g)

Tasty Tidbits

- Wasabi is a difficult plant to grow. It requires both a rocky stream and the proper mix of nutrients.

- Because of high demand for and limited supply of wasabi, some restaurants serve a mix of horseradish, mustard, and food coloring instead of the pure stuff.

SERVING SUGGESTION
Fruit "Sushi"

This fruity version of sushi calls for strawberries, blackberries, kiwi, and banana, but feel free to substitute any fruit you desire! You can also make the sushi with traditional sushi rice (as picured) if you prefer.

1 cup (235 ml) corn syrup

1 cup (150 g) brown sugar

1 cup (260 g) peanut butter

6 to 8 cups (85 to 112 g) puffed rice cereal

2 to 4 strawberries, sliced

2 to 4 blackberries, sliced

½ kiwi, peeled and sliced

1 banana, peeled and sliced

Seaweed, optional

In a saucepan over medium heat, bring corn syrup and brown sugar to a boil, stirring frequently.

Remove from heat and stir in peanut butter and puffed rice. Press into a greased 9 x 9-inch (23 x 23-cm) pan and let cool.

Cut out 1-inch (2.5-cm) circles from cereal treat (so they resemble rice rolls). Place sliced fruit combinations of your choice flat on each roll. To give an authentic sushi look, wrap in seaweed.

Yield: 9 pieces sushi

Cherry Blossom

Cherry blossom trees are indigenous to Asia and produce fragrant flowers which bloom for only a few days before falling. But this ice cream—perfect for a light, spring brunch—will bloom all year long.

1 cup (235 ml) soymilk, divided

2 tablespoons (16 g) arrowroot powder

2 cups (470 ml) soy creamer

¾ cup (150 g) sugar

1 tablespoon (15 ml) vanilla extract

1 tablespoon (15 ml) cherry blossom extract (purchase this at a specialty-food store or online)

½ cup (80 g) pitted black cherries, chopped

In a small bowl, combine ¼ cup (60 ml) soymilk with arrowroot and set aside.

Mix soy creamer, remaining ¾ cup (175 ml) soymilk, and sugar in a saucepan and cook over low heat. Once mixture begins to boil, remove from heat and immediately add arrowroot cream. This will cause the liquid to thicken noticeably.

Add vanilla and cherry blossom extracts.

Refrigerate mixture until chilled, approximately 2 to 3 hours. Freeze according to your ice cream maker's instructions. In the last few minutes of churning, add black cherries.

Yield: 1 quart (approximately 600 g)

Cashew Fruit

This sweet ice cream has a soft pink hue and a mild taste. Look for cashew fruit at a Brazilian market.

½ cup (50 g) raw cashew pieces

2 cups (470 ml) water, divided

1 tablespoon (15 ml) maple syrup

3 cashew fruits, peeled and sliced

2 tablespoons (16 g) arrowroot powder

1 cup (235 ml) soy creamer

½ cup (100 g) sugar

1 tablespoon (15 ml) vanilla extract

In a blender, combine cashew pieces with 1 cup (235 ml) water and maple syrup. Blend on high to form a thick cream. Slowly add remaining 1 cup (235 ml) water and blend on high for another 2 to 5 minutes. Pour into a medium-size bowl and set aside. This is your cashew milk.

In a food processor, blend sliced cashew fruits until smooth.

In a small bowl, mix ¼ cup (60 ml) freshly made cashew milk with arrowroot and set aside.

Mix soy creamer, remaining cashew milk, blended cashew fruits, and sugar in a saucepan and cook over low heat. Once mixture begins to boil, remove from heat and immediately add arrowroot cream. This will cause the liquid to thicken noticeably.

Add vanilla extract.

Refrigerate mixture until chilled, approximately 2 to 3 hours. Freeze according to your ice cream maker's instructions.

Yield: 1 quart (approximately 600 g)

Tasty Tidbit

- The cashew apple (or cashew fruit) is soft and pink. Its nuts—what we know as cashews—grow inside a shell attached to its skin. When on the tree, the fruit hangs with the nut at the bottom.

SERVING SUGGESTION

Spicy Fruit Salad

Peaches, bananas, and apples work well for this recipe, but feel free to use any fruit.

1 ripe peach, sliced

¼ cup (60 ml) orange juice

2 tablespoons (28 ml) dry white wine

¼ teaspoon ground cinnamon

Dash ground nutmeg

1 medium-size apple, cored and sliced

1 small banana, sliced

In a mixing bowl, combine peach slices, orange juice, wine, cinnamon, and nutmeg. Stir in apple and banana slices.

Cover and chill for 1 hour.

Yield: 3 to 4 cups (375 to 500 g)

Sweet Curry Fig

*Mild curries (yes, they do exist) intend to give diners a sophisticated food that offers a balanced blend of spices and herbs—much like this ice cream **(pictured at right)**.*

1 cup (235 ml) soymilk, divided

2 tablespoons (16 g) arrowroot powder

2 cups (470 ml) soy creamer

¾ cup (150 g) sugar

2 tablespoons (12 g) mild curry powder

1 tablespoon (15 ml) vanilla extract

20 fresh figs, chopped

In a small bowl, combine ¼ cup (60 ml) soymilk with arrowroot and set aside.

Mix soy creamer, remaining ¾ cup (175 ml) soymilk, sugar, and curry in a saucepan and cook over low heat. Once mixture starts to boil, remove from heat and immediately add arrowroot cream. This will cause the liquid to thicken noticeably. Add vanilla extract.

Refrigerate mixture until chilled, approximately 2 to 3 hours. Freeze according to your ice cream maker's instructions. In the last few minutes of churning, add chopped figs.

Yield: 1 quart (approximately 600 g)

Thai Chile Chocolate

There are many varieties of chile pepper, each varying in heat intensity. Choose one that suits your taste.

3 medium-size chile peppers, chopped

1 cup (235 ml) soymilk, divided

2 tablespoons (16 g) arrowroot powder

2 cups (470 ml) soy creamer

½ cup (100 g) sugar

¼ cup (20 g) cocoa powder

½ cup (90 g) vegan chocolate chips

1 tablespoon (15 ml) vanilla extract

In a blender, process chile peppers until smooth. Set aside.

In a small bowl, combine ¼ cup (60 ml) soymilk with arrowroot and set aside.

Mix soy creamer, blended chile peppers, remaining ¾ cup (175 ml) soymilk, sugar, cocoa powder, and chocolate chips in a medium saucepan over low heat. Stir frequently until chocolate chips melt, then bring mixture to a boil. Once it begins to boil, remove from heat and immediately add arrowroot cream. This will cause the liquid to thicken noticeably. Add vanilla extract.

Refrigerate mixture until chilled, approximately 2 to 3 hours. Freeze according to your ice cream maker's instructions.

Yield: 1 quart (approximately 600 g)

Tasty Tidbits

- Goji berries are a rich source oif vitamin C and fiber.

- The berries have been used in Tibet for at least 1,700 years, where they are believed to increase longevity, strength, and sexual potency.

Goji Berry Banana

Gogi berries come in several varieties. For this recipe, use the Himalayan version. They are larger and sweeter than their Chinese counterparts.

1½ cups (355 ml) water	2 cups (470 ml) soy creamer
1 cup (235 ml) soymilk, divided	¾ cup (150 g) sugar
2 tablespoons (16 g) arrowroot powder	1 tablespoon (15 ml) vanilla extract
3 bananas, peeled and sliced	½ cup (50 g) dried goji berries

In a small bowl, combine ¼ cup (60 ml) soymilk with arrowroot and set aside as well. In a blender, purée banana slices.

Mix soy creamer, puréed bananas, remaining ¾ cup (175 ml) soymilk, and sugar in a saucepan and cook over low heat. Once mixture begins to boil, remove from heat and immediately add arrowroot cream. This will cause the liquid to thicken noticeably.

Add vanilla extract.

Refrigerate mixture until chilled, approximately 2 to 3 hours. Freeze according to your ice cream maker's instructions. While the mixture is churning, soak goji berries in hot water for 5 minutes, until plump, then drain. In the last few minutes of churning, add goji berries.

Yield: 1 quart (approximately 600 g)

Red Bean

This ice cream is a unique translation of the popular red bean dishes common in Asian cuisine. Plus, it's a fun pink color! Look for red bean paste at Asian markets.

1 cup (235 ml) soymilk, divided

2 tablespoons (16 g) arrowroot powder

2 cups (470 ml) soy creamer

2 cups (525 g) red bean paste

¾ cup (150 g) sugar

1 tablespoon (15 ml) vanilla extract

In a small bowl, combine ¼ cup (60 ml) soymilk with arrowroot and set aside.

Mix soy creamer, remaining ¾ cup (175 ml) soymilk, bean paste, and sugar in a saucepan and cook over low heat. Once mixture begins to boil, remove from heat and immediately add arrowroot cream. This will cause the liquid to thicken noticeably.

Add vanilla extract.

Refrigerate mixture until chilled, approximately 2 to 3 hours. Freeze according to your ice cream maker's instructions.

Yield: 1 quart (approximately 600 g)

Tasty Tidbits

- The red bean is also called the adzuki bean.

- After the soybean, the red bean is the most popular bean in Japan.

SERVING SUGGESTION
Red Bean Pudding

This pudding is the perfect accompaniment to our Red Bean ice cream. Serve in bamboo-crafted bowls, if possible, for a complete Asian theme.

½ cup (85 g) red beans

2 pieces dried tangerine peel

2⅔ quarts (2.5 L) water

2 pandan leaves, knotted (purchase this at a specialty-food store, Asian market, or online)

½ cup (120 g) agave nectar

Wash red beans in several changes of water and remove grit that rises to surface. Rinse and drain. Rinse tangerine peel.

Bring water to a boil. Add red beans, pandan leaves, and tangerine peel and boil over high heat for 15 minutes. Lower heat and simmer for 1 hour, until beans are soft. Remove half of beans and blend until fine. Return blended bean paste to pot.

Add agave nectar and continue simmering over low heat for 30 minutes. Boil until mixture turns translucent and is a pudding-like consistency.

Yield: 2 cups (approximately 500 g)

Seaweed

Seaweed ice cream is popping up more and more in Eastern and Western ice cream shops. Serve with seaweed soaked in sugar syrup—or even Swedish fish candies—to complete the ocean theme.

3 to 4 ounces (85 to 115 g) fresh seaweed

1 cup (235 ml) water

1 cup (235 ml) soymilk, divided

2 tablespoons (16 g) arrowroot powder

2 cups (470 ml) soy creamer

¾ cup (150 g) sugar

1 tablespoon (15 ml) vanilla extract

Boil seaweed in water to break down any starchy branches, then blend drained seaweed until smooth (if not already smooth from boiling).

In a small bowl, combine ¼ cup (60 ml) soymilk with arrowroot and set aside.

Mix soy creamer, remaining ¾ cup (175 ml) soymilk, drained seaweed, and sugar in a saucepan and cook over low heat. Once mixture begins to boil, remove from heat and immediately add arrowroot cream. This will cause the liquid to thicken noticeably.

Add vanilla extract.

Refrigerate mixture until chilled, approximately 2 to 3 hours. Freeze according to your ice cream maker's instructions.

Yield: 1 quart (approximately 600 g)

Tasty Tidbits

- There are more than 9,000 known species of seaweed.

- Like other plants, seaweed depends on light for growth. For that reason, it occupies inner-tidal and other relatively shallow areas.

Green Fact

True or false? Ribofalvin is not an important part of a vegan diet. False. Ribofalvin, otherwise know as vitamin B2, converts protein, fat, and carbohydrates into energy. Good riboflavin sources include whole grains, leafy greens (seaweed included!), mushrooms, and almonds.

Almond Cookie

Chinese almond cookies are a popular treat at Chinese bakeries and a common part of Chinese New Year celebrations. This ice cream version is sure to be just as popular in your home!

1 cup (235 ml) almond milk, divided

2 tablespoons (16 g) arrowroot powder

2 cups (470 ml) soy creamer

¾ cup (150 g) sugar

1 tablespoon (15 ml) vanilla extract

4 to 5 Chinese almond cookies, crushed

In a small bowl, combine ¼ cup (60 ml) almond milk with arrowroot and set aside.

Mix soy creamer, remaining ¾ cup (175 ml) almond milk, and sugar in a saucepan and cook over low heat. Once mixture begins to boil, remove from heat and immediately add arrowroot cream. This will cause the liquid to thicken noticeably.

Add vanilla extract.

Refrigerate mixture until chilled, approximately 2 to 3 hours. Freeze according to your ice cream maker's instructions. In the last few minutes of churning, add crushed almond cookies.

Yield: 1 quart (approximately 600 g)

Tasty Tidbit

- The sweet almond was already in cultivation in China during the late Tang dynasty (618-906 AD), having been brought to the country from Russian Turkestan and central Asia.

Sweet Ginger Tea

This sweet-and-spicy ice cream is a natural metabolism booster. Serve with a dusting of cinnamon on top and a glass of iced ginger tea on the side. The pancakes below also pair perfectly.

1 cup (235 ml) soymilk, divided

2 tablespoons (16 g) arrowroot powder

2 cups (470 ml) soy creamer

½ cup (64 g) grated ginger root

¾ cup (150 g) sugar

1 tablespoon (15 ml) vanilla extract

In a small bowl, combine ¼ cup (60 ml) soymilk with arrowroot and set aside.

Mix soy creamer, remaining ¾ cup (175 ml) soymilk, ginger, and sugar in a saucepan and cook over low heat. Once mixture begins to boil, remove from heat and add arrowroot cream. This will cause the liquid to thicken noticeably.

Add vanilla extract.

Refrigerate mixture until chilled, approximately 2 to 3 hours. Freeze according to your ice cream maker's instructions.

Yield: 1 quart (approximately 600 g)

SERVING SUGGESTION
Fried Asian Pancakes

These light pancakes are best served warm, with fresh fruit and a scoop of ice cream.

1 tablespoon (8 g) white sesame seeds

1 cup (235 ml) water

1 tablespoon (7.5 g) ground flaxseed

¾ cup (95 g) all-purpose flour

3 tablespoons (45 ml) olive oil

Toast sesame seeds in frying pan over medium heat until fragrant, about 3 to 5 minutes, being careful not to let seeds burn. Remove from heat and set aside.

In a small bowl, whisk together water and ground flaxseed until slightly gelatinous, then gradually add flour. Stir in sesame seeds, mixing well until batter forms.

Heat oil in nonstick skillet over medium-high heat. Spoon batter into skillet and cook 2 to 3 minutes per side until light brown. Repeat with remaining batter.

Yield: 6 to 8 pancakes

Green Tea

Green tea—often described as fresh or light tasting—translates into a wonderfully refreshing ice cream. Add to that the health benefits of this flavor and you've got an irresistible one-two punch!

1 cup (235 ml) soymilk, divided

2 tablespoons (16 g) arrowroot powder

2 cups (470 ml) soy creamer

2 tablespoons (14 g) matcha (powdered Japanese green tea)

½ cup (100 g) sugar

1 tablespoon (15 ml) vanilla extract

In a small bowl, combine ¼ cup (60 ml) soymilk with arrowroot and set aside.

Mix soy creamer, remaining ¾ cup (175 ml) soymilk, matcha, and sugar in a saucepan and cook over low heat. Once mixture begins to boil, remove from heat and immediately add arrowroot cream. This will cause the liquid to thicken noticeably.

Add vanilla extract.

Refrigerate mixture until chilled, approximately 2 to 3 hours. Freeze according to your ice cream maker's instructions.

Yield: 1 quart (approximately 600 g)

Chocolate-Covered Raspberries

These little treats are simple to put together and make for a beautiful presentation.

3 ounces (84 g) semisweet or bittersweet chocolate, grated

2 tablespoons (28 ml) coconut milk

40 raspberries

Line a cake pan or a baking sheet with waxed paper (use a pan that will fit in your refrigerator).

Heat coconut milk in microwave for 10 to 15 seconds or on stovetop until bubbles start to form. Add grated chocolate and stir until smooth.

Drop a raspberry into chocolate, turn with a fork, lift out, and place on prepared pan. Don't worry about not coating entire berry. Repeat.

Chill until firm, at least 1 hour. Serve within 1 to 2 days.

Yield: 40 chocolate-covered raspberries

Tasty Tidbit

- Green tea is made from the same plant as teas such as black or oolong, but it's processed differently. Green tea is dried, not fermented.

Black Currant Tea

Black currant, typically used in wines, juices, and jams, gives this ice cream a rich, beautiful color. Serve with afternoon tea on a warm summer day.

1 cup (235 ml) soymilk, divided

2 tablespoons (16 g) arrowroot powder

1 cup (150 g) black currants

2 cups (470 ml) soy creamer

¾ cup (150 g) sugar

1 tablespoon (15 ml) vanilla extract

In a small bowl, combine ¼ cup (60 ml) soymilk with arrowroot and set aside.

In a blender, purée black currants, soy creamer, remaining ¾ cup (175 ml) soymilk, and sugar until smooth. Pour mixture into a saucepan and cook over low heat. Once it begins to boil, remove from heat and immediately add arrowroot cream. This will cause the liquid to thicken noticeably.

Add vanilla extract.

Refrigerate mixture until chilled, approximately 2 to 3 hours. Freeze according to your ice cream maker's instructions.

Yield: 1 quart (approximately 600 g)

Tasty Tidbit

- Black currants are a great source of anti-oxidants and vitamins, especially vitamin C.

SERVING SUGGESTION

Spicy Mango Salsa

This fruity salsa is delicious atop our Black Currant Tea ice cream or with organic tortilla chips.

1 large orange, peeled and diced

1 large, ripe mango, peeled, pitted, and diced

¼ cup (20 g) shredded coconut

2 tablespoons (28 ml) fresh lime juice

Pinch of cayenne pepper, optional

In a medium bowl, combine all ingredients. Toss to blend.

Yield: 1 ½ cups (375 g)

Eucalyptus

Eucalyptus is not just for koala bears anymore. Though we don't recommend eating the plant straight off of the tree, its oil offers a flavor that gives this savory ice cream a very clean and refreshing taste.

1 cup (235 ml) soymilk, divided

2 tablespoons (16 g) arrowroot powder

2 cups (470 ml) soy creamer

¾ cup (150 g) sugar

1 tablespoon (15 ml) vanilla extract

3 tablespoons (45 ml) eucalyptus extract (purchase this at a specialty-food store or online)

In a small bowl, combine ¼ cup (60 ml) soymilk with arrowroot and set aside.

Mix soy creamer, remaining ¾ cup (175 ml) soymilk, and sugar in a saucepan and cook over low heat. Once mixture begins to boil, remove from heat and immediately add arrowroot cream. This will cause the liquid to thicken noticeably.

Add vanilla and eucalyptus extracts.

Refrigerate mixture until chilled, approximately 2 to 3 hours. Freeze according to your ice cream maker's instructions.

Yield: 1 quart (approximately 600 g)

SERVING SUGGESTION

Raspberry Melba

Melba sauce was first created by the famous French chef Auguste Escoffier for Dame Nellie Melba, an Australian opera singer. This sweet specialty is a perfect ice cream topper.

1 teaspoon (2.7 g) cornstarch

⅛ teaspoon salt

¼ cup (85 g) agave nectar

1 cup (125 g) raspberries

½ cup (160 g) currant jelly

In a small bowl, mix cornstarch, salt, and agave nectar. Set aside.

Purée raspberries in a food processor and press mixture through a sieve to remove seeds. Discard solids.

Combine jelly and raspberry purée on top of a double boiler. Bring to a boil over medium heat.

Add cornstarch mixture to sauce, reduce to a simmer, and cook until thick and clear, about 10 minutes. Chill before serving.

Yield: 1¾ cups (560 g)

CHAPTER 5

Caribbean and Island Flavors

"A man travels the world in search of what he needs and returns home to find it."

—George Edward Moore, British philosopher

Pearly white beaches. Sky-blue water. Lush rain forests. When your surroundings are some of the most beautiful places in the world, you can't help but be inspired.

With cultural influences from Europe, Africa, and the Americas, the Caribbean islands have introduced the world to myriad unusual and exotic flavors. From cool coconut to sizzling spices, Caribbean cuisine offers something to satisfy anybody's taste.

I truly enjoyed designing these recipes because the process reminded me of working in my grandmother's kitchen in Jamaica. The smells and tastes brought back a wave of nostalgia. I hope these recipes inspire you to create your own memories!

Guava

Guavas have four times as much vitamin C as oranges. Plus, they give a beautiful hue to this ice cream.

½ cup (120 ml) soymilk, divided

2 tablespoons (16 g) arrowroot powder

4 guavas, peeled, seeded, and sliced

¼ cup (60 ml) almond milk

2 cups (470 ml) soy creamer

½ cup (100 g) sugar

1 tablespoon (15 ml) vanilla extract

In a small bowl, combine ¼ cup (60 ml) soymilk with arrowroot and set aside.

In a blender, combine sliced guava and almond milk until smooth.

Mix soy creamer, guava milk, remaining ¼ cup (60 ml) soymilk, and sugar in a saucepan and cook over low heat. Once mixture begins to boil, remove from heat and immediately add arrowroot cream. This will cause the liquid to thicken noticeably.

Add vanilla extract.

Refrigerate mixture until chilled, approximately 2 to 3 hours. Freeze according to your ice cream maker's instructions.

Yield: 1 quart (approximately 600 g)

Tasty Tidbits

- There are 150 guava varieties, ranging in size from 1 to 4 inches (2.5 to 10 cm).

- Guavas have anywhere from 100 to 500 small seeds, which, in some varieties, are edible.

SERVING SUGGESTION
Fig Purée

A "purée" is a light soup made from cooked fruits or vegetables blended in a food processor. This purée is best served warm, over ice cream.

1 tablespoon (14 g) non-hydrogenated, non-dairy butter

½ cup (120 ml) water

2 tablespoons (28 ml) lemon juice

1 tablespoon (20 g) agave nectar

1 tablespoon (15 ml) amaretto liqueur

¾ cup (120 g) coarsely chopped dried figs

Melt butter in a small saucepan over medium heat. Whisk in water, lemon juice, agave nectar, and amaretto liqueur until well combined.

Add figs, continuing to whisk. Cook for 6 to 8 minutes, until figs are plump and moist.

Transfer fig mixture to a food processor and blend until finely ground. Serve warm.

Yield: 2½ cups (approximately 600 ml)

Coconut

This refreshing, bright ice cream is a perfect summer treat. Sprinkle with grated coconut or brown sugar to serve.

3½ cups (825 ml) coconut milk, divided

2 tablespoons (16 g) arrowroot powder

¾ cup (150 g) sugar

1½ teaspoons (7.5 ml) vanilla extract

1½ teaspoons (7.5 ml) coconut extract

¾ cup (60 g) shredded coconut

In a small bowl, combine ¼ cup (60 ml) coconut milk with arrowroot and set aside.

Mix remaining 3¼ cups (765 ml) coconut milk and sugar in a saucepan, and cook over low heat. Once mixture begins to boil, remove from heat and immediately add arrowroot cream. This will cause the liquid to thicken noticeably.

Stir in vanilla and coconut extracts.

Refrigerate mixture until chilled, approximately 2 to 3 hours. Freeze according to your ice cream maker's instructions. In the last few minutes of churning, add shredded coconut.

Yield: 1 quart (approximately 600 g)

✳Variations: Coconut Cherry or Coconut Pineapple
To make Coconut Cherry ice cream, add ¾ cup (120 g) chopped black cherries in the last few minutes of churning. For Coconut Pineapple, mix in 1 cup (235 ml) pineapple juice before bringing ingredients to a boil.

Ginger Lychee

Lychee and ginger both have distinct flavors. One is very sweet, the other has a kick. Imagine the possibilities when you put the two together!

1 cup (235 ml) soymilk, divided

2 tablespoons (16 g) arrowroot powder

1 can lychees in syrup, for 1 cup (235 ml) syrup and 12 to 14 lychees, chopped

2 cups (470 ml) soy creamer

½ cup (64 g) grated ginger root

½ cup (100 g) sugar

1 tablespoon (15 ml) vanilla extract

In a small bowl, combine ¼ cup (60 ml) soymilk with arrowroot and set aside.

Mix lychee syrup, soy creamer, remaining ¾ cup (175 ml) soymilk, ginger root, and sugar in a saucepan and cook over low heat. Once mixture begins to boil, remove from heat and immediately add arrowroot cream. This will cause the liquid to thicken noticeably.

Add vanilla extract.

Refrigerate mixture until chilled, approximately 2 to 3 hours. Freeze according to your ice cream maker's instructions. In the last few minutes of churning, add chopped lychee fruit.

Yield: 1 quart (approximately 600 g)

SERVING SUGGESTION

Crispy Ginger Almond Wafer

For a gourmet dessert, serve Ginger Lychee ice cream on top of one of these wafesr.

1½ cups (180 g) powdered sugar

1¼ cups (155 g) all-purpose flour

½ cup (110 g) non-hydrogenated, non-dairy butter

1 tablespoon (6 g) minced and peeled fresh ginger

1 tablespoon (5.5 g) ground ginger

½ teaspoon ground cinnamon

½ teaspoon salt

¾ cup (110 g) whole almonds, toasted

3 tablespoons (11 g) whipped soy topping

3 tablespoons (42 g) chopped crystallized ginger

Preheat oven to 325°F (170°C or gas mark 3) and line two large baking sheets with parchment paper.

Combine sugar, flour, butter, fresh ginger, ground ginger, cinnamon, and salt in food processor and blend until mixture resembles coarse meal. Add almonds, whipped soy, and crystallized ginger and process until moist clumps form.

Shape dough into 1¼-inch (3-cm) balls and place on prepared sheets. Moisten bottom of a glass, dip into powder sugar, and press each dough ball to ¼-inch (½-cm) thickness.

Bake cookies until brown on bottom and edges, 25 to 28 minutes. Transfer to rack and cool.

Yield: 20 to 25 wafers

Tasty Tidbits

- Starfruit is rich in antioxidants and vitamin C, and low in sugar. Its taste has been described as a cross between a papaya and citrus fruit.

- Malaysia is the largest producer of starfruit.

Star Fruit

This fruit, which is both tart and sweet, acquired its name from its shape. No doubt this ice cream will be the star of your next dinner soirée.

1 cup (235 ml) soymilk, divided

2 tablespoons (16 g) arrowroot powder

4 to 5 star fruits, peeled, seeded, and chopped, divided

2 cups (470 ml) soy creamer

¾ cup (150 g) sugar

1 tablespoon (15 ml) vanilla extract

In a small bowl, combine ¼ cup (60 ml) soymilk with arrowroot and set aside.

In a food processor, purée half of chopped star fruit.

Combine puréed star fruit, soy creamer, remaining ¾ cup (175 ml) soymilk, and sugar in a saucepan and cook over low heat. Once mixture begins to boil, remove from heat and immediately add arrowroot cream. This will cause the liquid to thicken noticeably.

Add vanilla extract.

Refrigerate mixture until chilled, approximately 2 to 3 hours. Freeze according to your ice cream maker's instructions. In the last few minutes of churning, add remaining chopped star fruit.

Yield: 1 quart (approximately 600 g)

SERVING SUGGESTION

Watermelon Pineapple Ratatouille

Though typically a vegetable stew, "ratatouille" also can be made with fruit. This watermelon-pineapple variety goes great with any of the flavors in this chapter.

⅓ cup (80 ml) olive oil

1 pineapple, chopped

½ teaspoon basil

½ watermelon, chopped

Heat oil in a saucepan. Once hot, cook chopped pineapple for 2 to 3 minutes over high heat.

Add basil and chopped watermelon, and cook for 1 minute, stirring often. Serve warm, on ice cream.

Yield: 6 servings

Orange Passion Fruit

The tart flavor of passion fruit combined with the sweet taste of orange makes a delicious pair. Plus, both fruits are excellent sources of vitamin C. If you can't find fresh passion fruit, substitute ½ cup (125 g) canned passion fruit purée.

1 cup (235 ml) soymilk, divided

2 tablespoons (16 g) arrowroot powder

2 navel oranges

2 passion fruits, peeled, seeded, and sliced

2 cups (470 ml) soy creamer

¾ cup (150 g) sugar

1 tablespoon (15 ml) vanilla extract

In a small bowl, combine ¼ cup (60 ml) soymilk with arrowroot and set aside.

Finely grate 2 tablespoons (12 g) zest from oranges, then halve oranges and squeeze 1 cup (235 ml) juice. Discard oranges.

In a food processor, purée passion fruit until smooth.

Combine zest, orange juice, passion fruit purée, soy creamer, remaining ¾ cup (175 ml) soymilk, and sugar in a saucepan and cook over low heat. Once mixture begins to boil, remove from heat and immediately add arrowroot cream. This will cause the liquid to thicken noticeably.

Add vanilla extract.

Refrigerate mixture until chilled, approximately 2 to 3 hours. Freeze according to your ice cream maker's instructions.

Yield: 1 quart (approximately 600 g)

Tasty Tidbits

- There are two varieties of passion fruit: purple and yellow. The purple work better in this recipe and can be found in specialty markets.

- Passion fruit is a good source of vitamins A and C, potassium, and iron. One passion fruit has only 16 calories. When eaten with the seeds, it is an excellent source of fiber.

❋Variation: Orange Pineapple
Why not substitute pineapple for passion fruit? To create Orange Pineapple ice cream, use ½ a pineapple, peeled and chopped in place of the 2 passion fruits. The rest of the directions are the same!

Island-Green Pistachio

In Iran, pistachios are known as the "smiling nut." In China, they are called the "happy nut." One bite of this ice cream and we guarantee you'll be smiling in no time! Add a little hot fudge (page 202) on top and happiness is guaranteed.

1 cup (235 ml) soymilk, divided

2 tablespoons (16 g) arrowroot powder

1 cup shelled (120 g) pistachio nuts, divided

2 cups (470 ml) soy creamer

¾ cup (150 g) sugar

¼ teaspoon salt

1 tablespoon (15 ml) vanilla extract

In a small bowl, combine ¼ cup (60 ml) soymilk with arrowroot and set aside.

In a blender, purée ½ cup (60 g) pistachio nuts with ¼ cup (60 ml) soymilk.

Mix soy creamer, pistachio milk, remaining ½ cup (120 ml) soymilk, sugar, and salt in a saucepan and cook over low heat. Once mixture begins to boil, remove from heat and immediately add arrowroot cream. This will cause the liquid to thicken noticeably.

Add vanilla extract.

Refrigerate mixture until chilled, approximately 2 to 3 hours. Freeze according to your ice cream maker's instructions. In the last few minutes of churning, add remaining ½ cup (60 g) pistachio nuts.

Yield: 1 quart (approximately 600 g)

Tasty Tidbit

- Iran is the largest producer of pistachios in the world. The United States (namely, California) is the second.

Green Fact

Plant-based diets lower the rate of heart attacks by 85 percent and lower the cancer rate by 60 percent.

Key Lime

Key limes have a high juice content and are more tart and bitter than normal limes. Look for them in gourmet food stores—they are smaller than regular limes and more yellow in color than green. In this ice cream, they impart an incredible, unique flavor.

1 cup (235 ml) soymilk, divided

2 tablespoons (16 g) arrowroot powder

2 cups (470 ml) soy creamer

½ cup (120 ml) freshly squeezed key lime juice (about 2 to 3 limes worth, depending on size)

¾ cup (150 g) sugar

1 tablespoon (15 ml) vanilla extract

In a small bowl, combine ¼ cup (60 ml) soymilk with arrowroot and set aside.

Mix soy creamer, remaining ¾ cup (175 ml) soymilk, key lime juice, and sugar in a saucepan and cook over low heat. Once mixture begins to boil, remove from heat and immediately add arrowroot cream. This will cause the liquid to thicken noticeably.

Add vanilla extract.

Refrigerate mixture until chilled, approximately 2 to 3 hours. Freeze according to your ice cream maker's instructions.

Yield: 1 quart (approximately 600 g)

✳Variation: Strawberry or Raspberry Key Lime
In the last few minutes of churning, throw in ½ cup (85 g) chopped strawberries or whole raspberries.

Shandy

A "shandy," also known as a "radler" or a "panache," is typically a combination of beer and lemonade. Modeled after the drink, this sorbet is flavored with Caribbean lager and ginger.

½ cup (170 g) agave nectar

2 tablespoons (28 ml) ginger beer

2 tablespoons (28 ml) Caribbean lager

1 quart (940 ml) water

Combine all ingredients, then place mixture in ice cream maker and freeze according to its freezing instructions.

Yield: 1 quart (approximately 600 g)

Tasty Tidbit

- Shandy, founded in England, quickly spread to many British colonies. Outside of England, variations of the drink using locally available ingredients—ginger beer in the Caribbean, for example—started popping up.

SERVING SUGGESTION

Waffle Cones

Sophisticated ice cream calls for classy presentation. That's where these cones come in.
Note: You'll need a waffle iron to make them.

10 ounces (75 g) whipped soy topping

1 teaspoon (5 ml) vanilla extract

1½ cups (180 g) powdered sugar

1½ cups (185 g) all-purpose flour

¼ teaspoon ground cinnamon

1 tablespoon (8 g) cornstarch

Vegetable oil, for brushing waffle iron

In a medium-size bowl, combine soy topping with vanilla extract and whip thoroughly. Add remaining ingredients (except vegetable oil) and beat until mixture reaches batter-like consistency. Let sit for 30 minutes.

Heat up waffle cone iron and brush with oil. Pour batter into iron and bake until brown. Open iron, remove batter, and fold over a wooden cone, overlapping sides.

Yield: 30 cones

Caribbean Coffee

Instead of serving coffee with dessert, end dinner with a scoop of this ice cream served in coffee cups. For an authentic touch, add 1 tablespoon (14 ml) of rum along with the vanilla extract.

1 cup (235 ml) soymilk, divided

2 tablespoons (16 g) arrowroot powder

2 cups (470 ml) soy creamer

1 cup (235 ml) freshly brewed, strong Caribbean coffee

¾ cup (150 g) sugar

1 tablespoon (15 ml) vanilla extract

¼ cup (60 g) chocolate-covered coffee beans, optional

In a small bowl, combine ¼ cup (60 ml) soymilk with arrowroot and set aside.

Mix soy creamer, remaining ¾ cup (175 ml) soymilk, coffee, and sugar in a saucepan and cook over low heat. Once mixture begins to boil, remove from heat and immediately add arrowroot cream. This will cause the liquid to thicken noticeably. Stir in vanilla extract.

Refrigerate mixture until chilled, approximately 2 to 3 hours. Freeze according to your ice cream maker's instructions. In the last few minutes of churning, add chocolate-covered coffee beans, if desired.

Yield: 1 quart (approximately 600 g)

SERVING SUGGESTION

Pistachio Chocolate Biscotti

1 cup (125 g) all-purpose flour

½ cup (40 g) unsweetened cocoa powder

1 teaspoon (4.6 g) baking soda

¼ teaspoon salt

6 tablespoons (84 g) non-hydrogenated, non-dairy butter

1 cup (240 g) agave nectar

2 tablespoons (24 g) flaxseed

6 tablespoons (90 ml) water

1 cup (120 g) shelled pistachio nuts

½ cup (90 g) vegan chocolate chips

Preheat oven to 350°F (180°C or gas mark 4) and line a baking sheet with parchment paper.

In a medium-size bowl, whisk together flour, cocoa powder, baking soda, and salt.

In the bowl of an electric mixer, cream butter and agave nectar until light and fluffy. Add flaxseed and water, and beat until well combined (mixture may be slightly frothy). Scrape down sides of bowl every so often to ensure everything is well combined. Add flour mixture, and stir to form stiff dough. Stir in pistachios and chocolate chips.

Transfer dough to prepared baking sheet. Form into two logs, each 12 inches (30 cm) long by 4 inches (10 cm) wide. Bake until slightly firm, 22 to 25 minutes.

Cool for 5 minutes. Reduce oven to 300°F (150°C or gas mark 2).

Using a serrated knife, cut biscotti diagonally into 1-inch (2.5-cm) thick slices. Arrange evenly on baking sheet. Bake 10 minutes, turn over, and bake another 10 minutes or until firm to the touch. Remove from oven and let cool completely.

Yield: 40 biscotti

Dark-and-Stormy Sorbet

A Dark and Stormy's a tropical drink made exclusively with Gosling's Black Seal Rum and Bermuda Stone Ginger Beer. Stay true to the original drink when creating this tasty ice cream.

½ cup (170 g) agave nectar

2 tablespoons (28 ml) Gosling's Black Seal Rum

¼ cup (60 ml) Bermuda Stone Ginger Beer

1 quart (940 ml) water

Combine all ingredients, then place mixture in ice cream maker and freeze according to its freezing instructions.

Yield: 1 quart (approximately 600 g)

Ginger Beer Sorbet

This Caribbean-inspired sorbet tastes great in ginger beer floats.

½ cup (170 g) agave nectar

¼ cup (60 ml) ginger beer

1 quart (940 ml) water

Combine all ingredients, then place mixture in ice cream maker and freeze according to its freezing instructions.

Yield: 1 quart (approximately 600 g)

Green Fact

One person switching to a vegetarian diet saves more than 100 animals from industry cruelty each year.

CHAPTER 6

Novelty Flavors

"I am always doing that which I cannot do, in order that I may learn how to do it."

—Pablo Picasso

Life is all about trying new things, even in the kitchen!

I spent day after day, week after week trying to perfect these recipes, sometimes throwing my arms in the air and declaring myself too passionate. In the end, though, I think the flavors turned out amazingly delicious (you can judge for yourself)! Even in times of doubt, my determination kept me going.

I knew nothing about desserts when I first started making ice cream. Sheer resolve got me where I am today. So, if it worked for me, why not for you?

Try new things, play around with recipes, but most importantly, follow your passions. Life without risk is not worth living.

Pumpkin

This ice cream is a perfect treat for autumn.

1 cup (235 ml) soymilk, divided

2 tablespoons (16 g) arrowroot powder

2 cups (470 ml) soy creamer

¾ cup (113 g) brown sugar

1 cup (245 g) cooked, mashed pumpkin (or pumpkin purée)

2 tablespoons (14 g) pumpkin pie spice

1 tablespoon (15 ml) vanilla extract

In a small bowl, combine ¼ cup (60 ml) soymilk with arrowroot and set aside.

Mix soy creamer, remaining ¾ cup (175 ml) soymilk, brown sugar, pumpkin, and pumpkin pie spice in a saucepan and cook over low heat. Once mixture begins to boil, remove from heat and immediately add arrowroot cream. This will cause the liquid to thicken noticeably. Stir in vanilla extract.

Refrigerate mixture until chilled, approximately 2 to 3 hours. Freeze according to your ice cream maker's instructions.

Yield: 1 quart (approximately 600 g)

Tasty Tidbit

- The word pumpkin originates from the word *pepon*, which is Greek for "large melon."

SERVING SUGGESTION

Pie Crust Crumbles

2½ cups (310 g) all-purpose flour

1 teaspoon (6 g) salt

½ teaspoon agave nectar

1 cup (220 g) non-hydrogenated, non-dairy butter, cut into ½-inch (1-cm) cubes

4 to 6 tablespoons (60 to 90 ml) ice water

Preheat oven to 350°F (180°C or gas mark 4).

Combine flour, salt, and agave nectar in a food processor; pulse to mix. Add butter and pulse 6 to 8 times, until mixture resembles coarse meal. Add ice water 1 tablespoon (15 ml) at a time, pulsing until mixture begins to clump together. Dough is ready when it holds together when pinched.

Place dough in a mound on a clean surface and divide in half. Shape each half into a round, flat disk. Wrap each disk tightly with plastic wrap and refrigerate for at least 1 hour, or up to 2 days.

Remove one disk from refrigerator and let sit at room temperature for 5 to 10 minutes. On a lightly floured surface, roll into a 12-inch (30-cm) circle. You want it slightly larger than the pie pan so you can create a rim.

Line a pie pan with parchment or waxed paper. Transfer the dough to the pan, pressing to fit and trimming any edges. Fill pan at least two-thirds with dry beans, rice, or stainless-steel pie weights. Bake for 20 minutes.

Remove from oven, carefully remove pie weights, and let cool for a few minutes. With a fork, poke small holes in bottom of crust. Return to oven (without weights) and cook for an additional 10 minutes, until crust is golden. Once cooled, crush crust into pieces and sprinkle over ice cream.

Yield: Two 9-inch (23-cm) pie crusts

Chestnut

In preparation for making this flavorful ice cream, always slit the shells of chestnuts before cooking. This allows steam pressure to escape and prevents the nuts from bursting.

1 cup (235 ml) soymilk, divided

2 tablespoons (16 g) arrowroot powder

2 cups (470 ml) soy creamer

¾ cup (150 g) sugar

1 tablespoon (15 ml) vanilla extract

¾ cup (110 g) cooked and shelled chestnuts, chopped

In a small bowl, combine ¼ cup (60 ml) soymilk with arrowroot and set aside.

Mix soy creamer, remaining ¾ cup (175 ml) soymilk, and sugar in a saucepan and cook over low heat. Once mixture begins to boil, remove from heat and immediately add arrowroot cream. This will cause the liquid to thicken noticeably.

Add vanilla extract.

Refrigerate mixture until chilled, approximately 2 to 3 hours. Freeze according to your ice cream maker's instructions. In the last few minutes of churning, add chopped chestnuts.

Yield: 1 quart (approximately 600 g)

Tasty Tidbits

- A chestnut is a closed shell with moisture trapped inside. When heated, the moisture can forcefully pop open the nut. That's why it's important to slit a chestnut shell before cooking.

- There are many ways to cook chestnuts, including boiling, baking, and roasting. Any method will work here.

- To roast chestnuts, simply cut and "X" onto each nut's shell, place on a baking sheet, sprinkle with water, and roast for about 15 to 20 minutes at 425°F (220°C or gas mark 7).

Chocolate Pretzel

Looking for a salty-sweet treat? This winning combo is delicious. If you're feeling adventurous, try making your own chocolate-covered pretzels!

1 cup (235 ml) soymilk, divided

2 tablespoons (16 g) arrowroot powder

2 cups (470 ml) soy creamer

¾ cup (150 g) sugar

¼ cup (20 g) cocoa powder

½ cup (90 g) vegan chocolate chips

1 tablespoon (15 ml) vanilla extract

1½ cups (340 g) chopped chocolate-covered pretzels

In a small bowl, combine ¼ cup (60 ml) soymilk with arrowroot and set aside.

Mix soy creamer, remaining ¾ cup (175 ml) soymilk, sugar, cocoa powder, and chocolate chips in a medium-size saucepan over low heat. Stir frequently until chocolate chips melt, then bring mixture to a boil. Once it begins to boil, remove from heat and immediately add arrowroot cream. This will cause the liquid to thicken noticeably.

Add vanilla extract.

Refrigerate mixture until chilled, approximately 2 to 3 hours. Freeze according to your ice cream maker's instructions. In the last few minutes of churning, add chopped pretzels.

Yield: 1 quart (approximately 600 g)

✵Variation: Chocolate Pretzel Nut
Cashews or pecans would make a delicious addition to this sweet and salty treat. Simply reduce the pretzel pieces to 1 cup (225 g) and add ½ cup (55 g) chopped nuts along with the pretzels.

Avocado

This recipe works best with ripe avocados. That means the fruit should be a dark, greenish-black color and soft (almost mushy) to the touch. Because avocados contain natural binding agents, no arrowroot powder is required.

3 ripe avocados, peeled

1 tablespoon (15 ml) lime juice

½ cup (100 g) sugar

2 cups (470 ml) soy creamer

1 cup (235 ml) soymilk

In a blender, purée avocado flesh, lime juice, sugar, and soy creamer until smooth.

Pour purée into large bowl and add soymilk. Whisk until incorporated.

Place mixture into ice cream maker and freeze according to instructions.

Yield: 1 quart (approximately 600 g)

Tasty Tidbits

- Avocado is actually a fruit, not a vegetable.
- Avocados do not ripen until they are picked.

Cinnamon Juniper

This flavor combination is perfect for a winter holiday meal in front of a roaring fire. For an adult twist, serve with a splash of gin.

1 cup (235 ml) soymilk, divided

2 tablespoons (16 g) arrowroot powder

2 cups (470 ml) soy creamer

2 teaspoons (5 g) ground cinnamon

¾ cup (150 g) sugar

1 tablespoon (15 ml) vanilla extract

2 tablespoons (28 ml) juniper extract

In a small bowl, combine ¼ cup (60 ml) soymilk with arrowroot and set aside.

Mix soy creamer, remaining ¾ cup (175 ml) soymilk, cinnamon, and sugar in a saucepan and cook over low heat. Once mixture begins to boil, remove from heat and immediately add arrowroot cream. This will cause the liquid to thicken noticeably.

Add vanilla and juniper extracts.

Refrigerate mixture until chilled, approximately 2 to 3 hours. Freeze according to your ice cream maker's instructions.

Yield: 1 quart (approximately 600 g)

S'more

As the story goes, this American campfire delicacy owes its name to a troop of Girl Scouts. After tasting the warm marshmallow, melted chocolate, graham cracker combo, the girls chanted "Gimme some more!" and the name stuck. In no time, this unique ice cream will have you chanting those very same words.

1 cup (235 ml) soymilk, divided

2 tablespoons (16 g) arrowroot powder

2 cups (470 ml) soy creamer

¾ cup (150 g) sugar

¼ cup (20 g) cocoa powder

1½ cups (265 g) vegan chocolate chips, divided

1 tablespoon (15 ml) vanilla extract

1 cup (50 g) miniature marshmallows, lightly toasted

Vegan graham crackers, crumbled, for garnish

In a small bowl, combine ¼ cup (60 ml) soymilk with arrowroot and set aside.

Mix soy creamer, remaining ¾ cup (175 ml) soymilk, sugar, cocoa powder, and ½ cup (90 g) chocolate chips into a medium-size saucepan. On low heat, stir frequently until chocolate chips melt, then bring mixture to a boil. Once it begins to boil, remove from heat and immediately add arrowroot cream. This will cause the liquid to thicken noticeably.

Add vanilla extract.

Refrigerate mixture until chilled, approximately 2 to 3 hours. Freeze according to your ice cream maker's instructions. In the last few minutes of churning, add marshmallows and remaining chocolate chips. Garnish with crumbled graham crackers.

Yield: 1 quart (approximately 600 g)

Tasty Tidbit

- True graham crackers are made with unsifted and coarsely ground wheat flour. More similar in taste to a cookie than a cracker, they bear a resemblance—albeit a more square one—to the British "biscuit."

✳Variation: S'more Sandwiches
Simply place a scoop of S'more ice cream between two graham crackers and enjoy! Or, for an added treat, melt ½ cup (90 g) vegan chocolate chips and drizzle on bottom graham cracker layer before topping with ice cream.

Vanilla Graham Cracker

This ice cream tastes great with any flavor graham cracker. Try original, cinnamon, or chocolate.

1 cup (235 ml) soymilk, divided

2 tablespoons (16 g) arrowroot powder

2 cups (470 ml) soy creamer

¾ cup (150 g) sugar

1 tablespoon (15 ml) vanilla extract

1 cup (84 g) vegan graham crackers, crumbled and frozen

In a small bowl, combine ¼ cup (60 ml) soymilk with arrowroot and set aside.

Mix soy creamer, remaining ¾ cup (175 ml) soymilk, and sugar in a saucepan and cook over low heat. Once mixture begins to boil, remove from heat and immediately add arrowroot cream. This will cause the liquid to thicken noticeably. Add vanilla extract.

Refrigerate mixture until chilled, approximately 2 to 3 hours. Freeze according to your ice cream maker's instructions. In the last few minutes of churning, add frozen graham cracker bits.

Yield: 1 quart (approximately 600 g)

Tasty Tidbit

- Pure vanilla extract is made by macerating vanilla beans in an alcohol-water solution to extract the flavor. Imitation vanilla is composed entirely of artificial flavorings.

SERVING SUGGESTION

Ice Cream Cake

Enjoy this treat on birthdays, anniversaries, or any other special occasion.

3 cups (375 g) all-purpose flour

2 cups (400 g) sugar

½ cup (40 g) cocoa powder

2 teaspoons (9.2 g) baking soda

2 teaspoons (10 ml) vanilla extract

1 tablespoon (15 ml) vinegar

½ cup (120 ml) plus 2 tablespoons (28 ml) vegetable oil

2 cups (470 ml) water

10 to 15 vegan graham crackers, crushed

½ quart Vanilla Graham Cracker ice cream

Preheat oven to 350° F (180° C or gas mark 4).

Grease and flour two 9-inch (23-cm) round cake pans and set aside.

In a medium-size bowl, combine flour, sugar, cocoa powder, and baking soda. Stir in vanilla, vinegar, and oil. Add water and stir well.

Divide mixture evenly into cake pans, and bake for 30 to 35 minutes. Allow cakes to cool completely before removing from pans.

Put one cake on a serving platter. Spread ice cream over top and sprinkle with crushed graham crackers. Place remaining cake layer on top.

Place cake, uncovered, in freezer for several hours to firm up.

Yield: One 9-inch (23-cm) cake, 8 to 12 slices per cake

Cherry Pie

This sweet, cheerful ice cream is perfect for summer. For an even more authentic version, serve it with pie crust crumbles (see recipe on page 144) and a dollop of soy whipped cream.

1 cup (235 ml) almond milk, divided

2 tablespoons (16 g) arrowroot powder

2 cups (310 g) pitted cherries, quartered, divided

¾ cup (150 g) sugar

Splash of water

2 cups (470 ml) soy creamer

1 tablespoon (7 g) ground cinnamon

1 tablespoon (15 ml) vanilla extract

In a small bowl, combine ¼ cup (60 ml) almond milk with arrowroot and set aside.

Place 1¼ cup (195 g) pitted cherries and sugar in a medium-size saucepan. Add water and bring to a boil over low heat, stirring often. Once soft, purée cherries in a blender.

Mix soy creamer, remaining ¾ cup (175 ml) almond milk, and blended cherries in a saucepan and cook over low heat. Once mixture begins to boil, remove from heat and immediately add arrowroot cream. This will cause the liquid to thicken noticeably.

Add cinnamon and vanilla extract.

Refrigerate mixture until chilled, approximately 2 to 3 hours. Freeze according to your ice cream maker's instructions. In the last few minutes of churning, add remaining ¾ cup (115 g) chopped cherries.

Yield: 1 quart (approximately 600 g)

Tasty Tidbit

- Cherry pie is the second most popular pie in the United States. Apple pie is the most popular.

Green Fact

According to the Environmental Protection Agency, the runoff from factory farms pollutes our waterways more than all other industrial sources combined.

Apple Pie

In the nineteenth century, apple pie was commonly served for breakfast before a long day's work. Our Apple Pie ice cream may not be morning fare, but it is the perfect after-dinner treat.

For Apples:

3 apples, peeled, seeded, and chopped

2 tablespoons (14 g) ground cinnamon

1 cup (200 g) sugar

2 cups (470 ml) water

¼ cup (55 g) non-hydrogenated, non-dairy butter

For Ice Cream:

1 cup (235 ml) soymilk, divided

2 tablespoons (16 g) arrowroot powder

2 cups (470 ml) soy creamer

¾ cup (150 g) sugar

1 tablespoon (15 ml) vanilla extract

Cinnamon graham crackers, crushed, optional

To make apples: In a non-stick pan, combine apples, cinnamon, sugar, water, and butter, and bring to a boil on low heat. Cook until water evaporates, about 7 to 15 minutes. Remove from heat and set aside.

To make ice cream: In a small bowl, combine ¼ cup (60 ml) soymilk with arrowroot and set aside.

Mix soy creamer, remaining ¾ cup (175 ml) soymilk, cooked apples, and sugar in a saucepan and cook over low heat. Once mixture begins to boil, remove from heat and immediately add arrowroot cream. This will cause the liquid to thicken noticeably. Add vanilla extract.

Refrigerate mixture until chilled, approximately 2 to 3 hours. Freeze according to your ice cream maker's instructions. Garnish with crushed cinnamon graham crackers, if desired.

Yield: 1 quart (approximately 600 g)

Pecan Apple Danish

Apples can be found year round, but are quintessentially an autumn treat, with their peak season from September through November. Add a twist to your typical fall dessert with this homey flavor.

For Apples:

3 apples, peeled, seeded, and chopped

2 tablespoons (14 g) ground cinnamon

1 cup (200 g) sugar

2 cups (470 ml) water

¼ cup (55 g) non-hydrogenated, non-dairy butter

For Ice Cream:

1 cup (235 ml) soymilk, divided

2 tablespoons (16 g) arrowroot powder

2 cups (470 ml) soy creamer

¾ cup (113 g) brown sugar

1 tablespoon (15 ml) vanilla extract

½ cup (55 g) chopped pecans

4 to 5 pieces vegan Danish bread, optional

To make apples: In a non-stick pan, combine apples, cinnamon, sugar, water, and butter, and bring to a boil. Cook until water evaporates, about 7 to 15 minutes. Remove from heat and set aside.

To make ice cream: In a small bowl, combine ¼ cup (60 ml) soymilk with arrowroot and set aside.

Mix soy creamer, remaining ¾ cup (175 ml) soymilk, cooked apples, and brown sugar in a saucepan and cook over low heat. Once mixture begins to boil, remove from heat and immediately add arrowroot cream. This will cause the liquid to thicken noticeably. Add vanilla extract.

Refrigerate mixture until chilled, approximately 2 to 3 hours. Freeze according to your ice cream maker's instructions. In the last few minutes of churning, add chopped pecans. Serve with Danish bread, if desired.

Yield: 1 quart (approximately 600 g)

Vanilla Saffron

Saffron has a unique, bitter, honey-like taste that makes for a luxurious ice cream. Don't let the price tag on this expensive spice (up to $1,200 [£760] per pound [454 g]) deter you. It's worth the cost.

1 cup (235 ml) soymilk, divided

2 tablespoons (16 g) arrowroot powder

2 cups (470 ml) soy creamer

¼ cup (8 g) saffron spice

¾ cup (150 g) sugar

1 tablespoon (15 ml) vanilla extract

In a small bowl, combine ¼ cup (60 ml) soymilk with arrowroot and set aside.

Mix soy creamer, saffron, remaining ¾ cup (175 ml) soymilk, and sugar in a saucepan and cook over low heat. Once mixture begins to boil, remove from heat and immediately add arrowroot cream. This will cause the liquid to thicken noticeably. Add vanilla extract.

Refrigerate mixture until chilled, approximately 2 to 3 hours. Freeze according to your ice cream maker's instructions.

Yield: 1 quart (approximately 600 g)

Tasty Tidbits

- Although Iran produces the majority of the world's saffron, Spain is the world's largest exporter of the spice.

- In large doses (more than ½ cup [17 g]), saffron is lethal.

SERVING SUGGESTION

Roasted Peaches

Delicately roasted peaches with a sprinkle of brown sugar accompany this ice cream perfectly.

6 medium peaches

2 tablespoons (28 g) non-hydrogenated, non-dairy butter, softened

2½ tablespoons (52 g) agave nectar

Brown sugar, for garnish

Preheat oven to 325°F (170°C or gas mark 3).

Slice each peach into 8 pieces and place on pan with foil. Combine butter and agave nectar in a saucepan and cook over low heat until butter melts. Brush tops of peaches with butter-agave mixture.

Roast for 10 to 15 minutes, until peaches are soft. Sprinkle with brown sugar and serve.

Yield: 10 servings

Sweet Potato

Don't confuse sweet potatoes, this recipe's main ingredient, with yams. Nutritionally, the former greatly outweighs the latter. This fun dessert is perfect for autumn banquets.

For Sweet Potatoes:

4 to 5 sweet potatoes

½ cup (100 g) sugar

2 to 4 teaspoons (5 to 9 g) ground nutmeg

Dash of salt

For Ice Cream:

1 cup (235 ml) soymilk, divided

2 tablespoons (16 g) arrowroot powder

2 cups (470 ml) soy creamer

¾ cup (150 g) sugar

1 tablespoon (15 ml) vanilla extract

To make sweet potatoes: Bake potatoes at 400°F (200°C or gas mark 6) for 40 to 50 minutes. Mash and add sugar, nutmeg, and salt. Let cool.

To make ice cream: In a small bowl, combine ¼ cup (60 ml) soymilk with arrowroot and set aside.

Mix soy creamer, remaining ¾ cup (175 ml) soymilk, and sugar in a saucepan and cook over low heat. Once mixture begins to boil, remove from heat and immediately add arrowroot cream. This will cause the liquid to thicken noticeably. Add vanilla extract.

Refrigerate both mixtures until chilled, approximately 2 to 3 hours. Combine and freeze according to your ice cream maker's instructions.

Yield: 1 quart (approximately 600 g)

SERVING SUGGESTION

Slow-Roasted Green Apples

1 tablespoon (7 g) ground cinnamon

¼ cup (85 g) agave nectar

2 large Fuji apples, peeled and cut into ¼-inch (½-cm) slices

¼ cup (60 ml) apple juice

2 tablespoons (25 g) sugar

Combine cinnamon and agave nectar in a medium-size bowl. Add apple slices to bowl and toss to coat.

Preheat oven to 375°F (190°C or gas mark 5).

Combine apple juice with sugar in a medium-size pan over medium heat. Cook for 3 to 4 minutes, until sugar dissolves and a light syrup forms.

Add coated apple slices to the syrup. Heat for 2 minutes, spooning syrup over apples to coat evenly. Turn mixture onto an ungreased, rimmed baking pan and bake for 8 minutes, or until apples are slightly firm but easily pierced with a sharp knife. Let apples sit in pan to cool.

To serve, fan out sliced apple halves on individual plates or in bowls. Top with a scoop of ice cream and spoon syrup mixture from pan on top of ice cream, if desired.

Yield: 4 servings

New York Irish Cream

Serve this ice cream at your next St. Patrick's Day bash! For even more festive Irish flair, add a few drops of green food coloring.

1 cup (235 ml) soymilk, divided

2 tablespoons (16 g) arrowroot powder

2 cups (470 ml) soy creamer

¾ cup (150 g) sugar

1 tablespoon (15 ml) vanilla extract

½ cup (170 g) agave nectar

2 tablespoons (28 ml) whiskey

In a small bowl, combine ¼ cup (60 ml) soymilk with arrowroot and set aside.

Mix soy creamer, remaining ¾ cup (175 ml) soymilk, and sugar in a saucepan and cook over low heat. Once mixture begins to boil, remove from heat and immediately add arrowroot cream. This will cause the liquid to thicken noticeably.

Add vanilla extract and agave nectar.

Refrigerate mixture until chilled, approximately 2 to 3 hours. Freeze according to your ice cream maker's instructions. In the last few minutes of churning, add whiskey.

Yield: 1 quart (approximately 600 g)

Tasty Tidbit

- Irish cream is a mixture of whiskey, cream, and sugar. It is typically sold preblended and nearly always uses Irish whiskey as its base.

Green Fact

Two-thirds of the ammonia emitted worldwide comes from farming animals. Ammonia emission significantly contributes to acid rain and global warming. Following a vegan or vegetarian diet can reduce these detriments to our environment.

Host an Ice Cream Tasting Party

Like wine, a great ice cream is complex and deep, with bright flavors and luscious undertones. In fact, the cacao we use at the store in our classic Chocolate has 300 more flavor components than a glass of your favorite wine.

Here's a step-by-step guide to host the perfect ice cream tasting party. Your friends will be ice cream connoisseurs in no time!

Step 1: Decide which flavors to offer.

If you're a beginner, stick with the classics: Vanilla (page 36), Chocolate (page 37), and Strawberry (page 46). If you're an old pro, impress your guests with fancier flavors such as Raspberry Dandelion (page 100), Seaweed (page 119), and Espresso Bean (page 164).

Like a wine tasting, move from lightest to darkest shade of ice cream.

Step 2: Set out the good stuff.

A true ice cream virtuoso always uses a gold spoon when sampling a new flavor. However, if you don't have any gold spoons on hand, silver spoons work just as well and will not alter delicate flavors. Never use plastic or wooden spoons, as they tend to leave a slight aftertaste.

Step 3: Keep your mouth clean.

The human palate consists of more than 9,000 taste buds. To cleanse your palate before the sampling begins and between each flavor, rinse your mouth with lukewarm water and eat one half of a plain, unsalted cracker. This will clear any traces of previously consumed food or drink.

Step 4: Let the ice cream sit.

For maximum flavor release, temper your ice cream by leaving it out for 10 to 15 minutes. Or, for a quick fix, microwave the container for 10 seconds.

Step 5: Judge weight and body.

Do this by lifting the ice cream container with one hand. For its size, is it heavy or light? Gourmet ice cream (yours!) should feel remarkably heavy due to the process in which it is made. Commercial ice cream is typically pretty light because of large amounts of air whipped into the mixture as the ice cream freezes.

Step 6: Observe how it looks.

Scoop up a spoonful of ice cream and carefully observe its appearance. Is it a natural, enticing hue? Premium ice cream should feature decadent colors and flecks of flavoring. Ice cream specialists claim that a taster should be able to "see" the top note of flavor (the smell and the first taste senses pick up) in the first spoonful.

Step 7: Give it a sniff.

Believe it or not, artisanal ice cream will have a slight, subtle bouquet. Lift the spoon and smell the ice cream. It may be hard to detect, but the scent will subtly hint at the flavor notes in the ice cream.

Step 8: Go for direct contact.

Invert the spoon and place it into your mouth, so the ice cream—rather than the bottom of a cold spoon—is the first thing your tongue will touch. Close your eyes. Is the flavor released quickly or does it build? What is your first impression?

Step 9: Explore the flavors.

As the ice cream melts and leaves your mouth, the finishing flavors (after taste) arise. Are they stronger or completely different than the first flavors? Our Sweet Curry Fig ice cream (page 114), for example, begins sweet but finishes with a strong, spicy kick. It is during this important step that most people judge whether they enjoy an ice cream flavor.

Step 10: Explore the feel.

The first spoonful is an intimate connection with the flavor. Use the second spoonful to test the texture and consistency of the ice cream. Is it creamy? Are there grains of flavor in each bite? Can you chew the ice cream, or does it immediately yield and melt in your mouth?

Step 11: Give your opinion.

Record or discuss your results (you can even use a rating system, using "scoops" instead of stars).

Step 12: Enjoy!

Spend your time enjoying the ice cream while relaxing and socializing with friends. You are now a true ice cream connoisseur!

Apple Cider

Apple cider bought in a supermarket is pasteurized, which prevents fermentation. Cider fresh from a farm or roadside stand is unpasteurized (which allows for fermentation in the bottle) and usually has a more pronounced flavor and fizzy taste. Both work well for this recipe.

1 cup (235 ml) soymilk, divided

2 tablespoons (16 g) arrowroot powder

1 cup (235 ml) organic apple cider

2 cups (470 ml) soy creamer

¾ cup (150 g) sugar

1 tablespoon (15 ml) vanilla extract

In a small bowl, combine ¼ cup (60 ml) soymilk with arrowroot and set aside.

Combine apple cider, soy creamer, remaining ¾ cup (175 ml) soymilk, and sugar in a saucepan and cook over low heat. Once mixture begins to boil, remove from heat and immediately add arrowroot cream. This will cause the liquid to thicken noticeably.

Add vanilla extract.

Refrigerate mixture until chilled, approximately 2 to 3 hours. Freeze according to your ice cream maker's instructions.

Yield: 1 quart (approximately 600 g)

Green Fact

In the fight against global warming, adopting a vegan diet has a greater impact than switching to a hybrid car, according to a 2006 report from the University of Chicago.

Lemonade

This ice cream is best enjoyed on the front porch on a hot, summer night. Squeeze fresh lemon juice on top for a stronger citrus flavor.

1 cup (235 ml) soymilk, divided

2 tablespoons (16 g) arrowroot powder

1½ cups (355 ml) lemonade (freshly made is best)

2 cups (470 ml) soy creamer

¾ cup (150 g) sugar

1 tablespoon (15 ml) vanilla extract

In a small bowl, combine ¼ cup (60 ml) soymilk with arrowroot and set aside.

Combine lemonade, soy creamer, remaining ¾ cup (175 ml) soymilk, and sugar in a saucepan and cook over low heat. Once mixture begins to boil, remove from heat and immediately add arrowroot cream. This will cause the liquid to thicken noticeably.

Add vanilla extract.

Refrigerate mixture until chilled, approximately 2 to 3 hours. Freeze according to your ice cream maker's instructions.

Yield: 1 quart (approximately 600 g)

Tasty Tidbits

- Lemons are originally from northern India.

- Lemonade is believed to have been invented in Egypt more than 1,500 years ago. It started as a lemon and honey wine, drank primarily by peasants.

SERVING SUGGESTION
Strawberry Salad

This bountiful salad, packed with nutrient-rich fruits, goes great with Lemonade ice cream or any of the fruit-flavored ice creams from chapter 2.

1 quart (580 g) strawberries, chopped

2 oranges, peeled and sliced

1 pineapple, peeled and chopped

1 avocado, peeled and chopped

1 pint (290 g) blueberries

Lime juice, to taste

Mix fruit in a bowl. Add lime juice to taste.

Yield: 5 to 6 cups (850 to 1020 g)

Bourbon Raisin

This recipe may be a little too sophisticated for the kids, but it's great for an adults-only evening. For a charming Southern flavor, use your favorite Kentucky bourbon.

1 cup (235 ml) soymilk, divided

2 tablespoons (16 g) arrowroot powder

2 cups (470 ml) soy creamer

¾ cup (150 g) sugar

1 tablespoon (15 ml) vanilla extract

2 tablespoons (28 ml) bourbon

¾ cup (110 g) raisins

In a small bowl, combine ¼ cup (60 ml) soymilk with arrowroot and set aside.

Mix soy creamer, remaining ¾ cup (175 ml) soymilk, and sugar in a saucepan and cook over low heat. Once mixture begins to boil, remove from heat and immediately add arrowroot cream. This will cause the liquid to thicken noticeably.

Add vanilla extract.

Refrigerate mixture until chilled, approximately 2 to 3 hours. Freeze according to your ice cream maker's instructions. In the last few minutes of churning, add bourbon and raisins.

Yield: 1 quart (approximately 600 g)

Prune Armagnac Sorbet

Armagnac is a distinctive eau-de-vie (colorless fruit brandy) made from aged grapes. It produces quite the debonair sorbet, for those of worldly status.

½ cup (170 g) agave nectar

2 tablespoons (28 ml) armagnac

1½ tablespoons (23 ml) prune juice

1 quart (940 ml) water

Combine all ingredients. Place mixture in ice cream maker and freeze according to instructions.

Yield: 1 quart (approximately 600 g)

Earl Grey

Bergamot oranges flavor Earl Grey tea and give this ice cream its unique flavor. Serve with crumpets and cucumber sandwiches. Cheers!

1 cup (235 ml) soymilk, divided

2 tablespoons (16 g) arrowroot powder

2 cups (470 ml) soy creamer

¾ cup (150 g) sugar

8 bags Earl Grey tea

1 tablespoon (15 ml) vanilla extract

In a small bowl, combine ¼ cup (60 ml) soymilk with arrowroot and set aside.

Mix soy creamer, remaining ¾ cup (175 ml) soymilk, and sugar in a saucepan and bring to a boil over medium heat. Place teabags in mixture and steep for 20 minutes.

Remove teabags, then heat mixture over medium-low heat. Once mixture begins to boil, remove from heat and immediately add arrowroot cream. This will cause the liquid to thicken noticeably.

Add vanilla extract.

Refrigerate mixture until chilled, approximately 2 to 3 hours. Freeze according to your ice cream maker's instructions.

Yield: 1 quart (approximately 600 g)

Green Fact

It takes 78 calories of fossil fuel to produce 1 calorie of meat protein. It takes 1 calorie of fossil fuel to produce 1 calorie of plant-based protein. By following a vegan diet, you conserve non-renewable sources of energy.

Tasty Tidbits

- Traditionally, Earl Grey tea was a blend of black teas from China and natural bergamot oil, taken from the bergamot tree. This citrus fruit gave the tea it's famously perfumed aroma and flavor. Today, Earl Grey is likely made with Indian and Sri Lankan black tea.

- The original blend of Earl Grey tea was created for British Prime Minister Charles Grey, Second Earl Grey. Legend has it he received the blend as a gift from a Chinese mandarin.

Espresso Bean

The rich candy-coated beans in this recipe provide a wonderful contrast to the smooth vanilla flavor of this ice cream.

Tasty Tidbit

- Espresso beans differ from regular coffee bean in that they are roasted longer, so that the oils are brought to the bean's surface.

1 cup (235 ml) soymilk, divided

2 tablespoons (16 g) arrowroot powder

2 cups (470 ml) soy creamer

¾ cup (150 g) sugar

1 tablespoon (15 ml) vanilla extract

¾ cup (180 g) vegan chocolate-covered espresso beans

In a small bowl, combine ¼ cup (60 ml) soymilk with arrowroot and set aside.

Mix soy creamer, remaining ¾ cup (175 ml) soymilk, and sugar in a saucepan and cook over low heat. Once mixture begins to boil, immediately add arrowroot cream. This will cause the liquid to thicken noticeably.

Add vanilla extract.

Refrigerate mixture until chilled, approximately 2 to 3 hours. Freeze according to your ice cream maker's instructions. In the last few minutes of churning, add chocolate-covered espresso beans.

Yield: 1 quart (approximately 600 g)

SERVING SUGGESTION

Hot Chocolate Fondant

A "fondant" is a sweet, thick icing made from cooking sugar, water, and syrup (or cream of tartar). Once cooked and cooled, it can be kneaded into a pliable consistency and used to decorate cakes. Heating fondant, on the other hand, makes it soft enough to be used as ice cream coating.

3 cups (1020 g) agave nectar

5 ounces (150 ml) water

2 tablespoons (28 ml) light corn syrup

3 ounces (84 g) unsweetened chocolate, chopped

1 teaspoon (5 ml) almond extract

In a saucepan, combine agave nectar, water, and corn syrup. Cook over low heat, stirring constantly, until mixture cooks down and reaches 92°F (33°C).

Remove from heat and stir in chopped chocolate and almond extract, until chocolate melts and mixture is smooth. Spoon warm fondant over ice cream.

Yield: 1½ cups (355 ml)

Cappuccino

Cappuccino is a drink made of equal parts espresso, steamed milk, and frothed milk. The drink's many layers make for a multifaceted treat.

Tasty Tidbits

- A cappuccino differs from a latté in that the former has less steamed milk than the latter.

- In Italy, cappuccino is often served in the morning, as part of breakfast.

For Cappuccino:

1 tablespoon (15 ml) instant espresso

2 teaspoons (3 g) cocoa powder

½ teaspoon ground cinnamon

½ cup (100 g) sugar

¼ cup (60 ml) boiling water

For Ice Cream:

1 cup (235 ml) soymilk, divided

2 tablespoons (16 g) arrowroot powder

2 cups (470 ml) soy creamer

½ cup (100 g) sugar

1 tablespoon (15 ml) vanilla extract

To make cappuccino: Combine espresso, cocoa powder, cinnamon, and sugar. Stir in boiling water. Let mixture cool.

To make ice cream: In a small bowl, combine ¼ cup (60 ml) soymilk with arrowroot and set aside.

Mix soy creamer, cappuccino, remaining ¾ cup (175 ml) soymilk, and sugar in a saucepan and cook over low heat. Once mixture begins to boil, remove from heat and immediately add arrowroot cream. This will cause the liquid to thicken noticeably. Add vanilla extract.

Refrigerate mixture until chilled, approximately 2 to 3 hours. Freeze according to your ice cream maker's instructions.

Yield: 1 quart (approximately 600 g)

Espresso

Inspired by the strong Italian coffee drink, this ice cream plays well with those who love a jolt of caffeine in their dessert.

1 cup (235 ml) soymilk, divided

2 tablespoons (16 g) arrowroot powder

2 cups (470 ml) soy creamer

¾ cup (175 ml) fresh, strong espresso

¾ cup (150 g) sugar

1 tablespoon (15 ml) vanilla extract

In a small bowl, combine ¼ cup (60 ml) soymilk with arrowroot and set aside.

Mix soy creamer, remaining ¾ cup (175 ml) soymilk, espresso, and sugar in a saucepan and cook over low heat. Once mixture begins to boil, remove from heat and immediately add arrowroot cream. This will cause the liquid to thicken noticeably. Add vanilla extract.

Refrigerate mixture until chilled, approximately 2 to 3 hours. Freeze according to your ice cream maker's instructions.

Yield: 1 quart (approximately 600 g)

Brown Sugar Caramel

This sugary ice cream is sure to please any sweet tooth.

1 cup (235 ml) soymilk, divided

2 tablespoons (16 g) arrowroot powder

2 cups (470 ml) soy creamer

1 cup (150 g) brown sugar

1 tablespoon (15 ml) vanilla extract

¾ cup (170 g) vegan caramel

In a small bowl, combine ¼ cup (60 ml) soymilk with arrowroot and set aside.

Mix soy creamer, remaining ¾ cup (175 ml) soymilk, and brown sugar in a saucepan and cook over low heat. Once mixture begins to boil, remove from heat and immediately add arrowroot cream. This will cause the liquid to thicken noticeably. Add vanilla extract.

Refrigerate mixture until chilled, approximately 2 to 3 hours. Freeze according to your ice cream maker's instructions. In the last few minutes of freezing, heat up caramel (either in the microwave or on the stove) and swirl through ice cream.

Refrigerate mixture until chilled, approximately 2 to 3 hours. Freeze according to your ice cream maker's instructions.

Yield: 1 quart (approximately 600 g)

Granola Crunch

Granola, finally a mainstream snack after maintaining its hippie reputation for years, is a great addition to ice cream. Homemade granola is the best, but if you must purchase from a supermarket, beware of brands that use honey.

Tasty Tidbit

- Granola was invented in 1863 by Dr. James C. Jackson who advocated the mixture as part of a healthy diet. The original version consisted of broken-up and re-baked pieces of graham flour crackers.

1 cup (235 ml) soymilk, divided

2 tablespoons (16 g) arrowroot powder

2 cups (470 ml) soy creamer

¾ cup (150 g) sugar

1 tablespoon (15 ml) vanilla extract

1 cup (80 g) granola

In a small bowl, combine ¼ cup (60 ml) soymilk with arrowroot and set aside.

Mix soy creamer, remaining ¾ cup (175 ml) soymilk, and sugar in a saucepan and cook over low heat. Once mixture begins to boil, remove from heat and immediately add arrowroot cream. This will cause the liquid to thicken noticeably.

Add vanilla extract.

Refrigerate mixture until chilled, approximately 2 to 3 hours. Freeze according to your ice cream maker's instructions. In the last few minutes of churning, add granola.

Yield: 1 quart (approximately 600 g)

SERVING SUGGESTION

Spicy Cherry Salsa

The jalapeños in this recipe balance out the sweet cherry and citrus lime flavors.
Serve cold, over ice cream, or with homemade tortilla chips.

1 cup (155 g) pitted dark sweet cherries, chopped

1 tablespoon (15 ml) lime juice

¼ cup (80 g) cherry preserves

1 teaspoon (3 g) finely chopped jalapeño pepper

Combine all ingredients in medium-size bowl and stir to blend. Cover and chill for 1 to 2 hours before serving.

Yield: 1½ cups (375 g)

Peanut Butter Banana

Inspired by the favorite after-school snack, this ice cream is perfect any time of the day.

3 ripe bananas

2 cups (470 ml) soymilk

¾ cup (113 g) brown sugar

¾ cup (195 g) peanut butter

1 tablespoon (15 ml) vanilla extract

Peel bananas. In a food processor, purée bananas and soymilk until smooth.

Transfer liquid to a medium-size saucepan. Add brown sugar and peanut butter and cook over low heat until sugar dissolves. Remove from heat and add vanilla extract, stirring to combine.

Refrigerate mixture until chilled, approximately 2 to 3 hours. Freeze according to your ice cream maker's instructions.

Yield: 1 quart (approximately 600 g)

Banana Molasses

Much like sugar, molasses acts as a sweetener. When it's mixed with bananas, as in this recipe, the result is a creamy ice cream that goes well with chocolate syrup.

2 ripe bananas, peeled and sliced

1¼ cups (295 ml) soymilk, divided

2 tablespoons (16 g) arrowroot powder

2 cups (470 ml) soy creamer

½ cup (120 g) regular molasses

¼ cup (60 g) blackstrap molasses

1 tablespoon (15 ml) vanilla extract

Peel bananas. In a food processor, purée bananas and ¼ cup (60 ml) soymilk until smooth.

In a small bowl, combine ¼ cup (60 ml) soymilk with arrowroot and set aside.

Mix soy creamer, banana-milk mixture, remaining ¾ cup (175 ml) soymilk, and both types of molasses in a saucepan and cook over low heat. Once mixture begins to boil, remove from heat and immediately add arrowroot cream. This will cause the liquid to thicken noticeably.

Add vanilla extract.

Refrigerate mixture until chilled, approximately 2 to 3 hours. Freeze according to your ice cream maker's instructions.

Yield: 1 quart (approximately 600 g)

Peanut Butter and Jelly

*This flavor (**pictured at left**) tastes just like the sandwich. It's sure to be a real hit with kids and those who are young at heart!*

1 cup (235 ml) soymilk

2 cups (470 ml) soy creamer

¾ cup (195 g) peanut butter

¾ cup (113 g) brown sugar

1 tablespoon (15 ml) vanilla extract

¾ cup (240 g) jam, jelly, or preserves of preference

Mix soymilk, soy creamer, peanut butter, and brown sugar in a saucepan and cook over low heat. Once mixture begins to boil, remove from heat. Add vanilla extract.

Refrigerate mixture until chilled, approximately 2 to 3 hours. Freeze according to your ice cream maker's instructions. In the last few minutes of churning, add jam.

Yield: 1 quart (approximately 600 g)

Peanut Butter Cucumber

Cucumbers add a crisp, refreshing flavor to this smooth, creamy ice cream. Seedless cucumber chunks are your best bet.

4 to 5 cucumbers, peeled, seeded, and chopped

1 cup (235 ml) soymilk, divided

2 tablespoons (16 g) arrowroot powder

2 cups (470 ml) soy creamer

¾ cup (113 g) brown sugar

1 tablespoon (15 ml) vanilla extract

½ cup (130 g) peanut butter

In a blender, purée cucumber chunks.

In a small bowl, combine ¼ cup (60 ml) soymilk with arrowroot and set aside.

Mix soy creamer, remaining ¾ cup (175 ml) soymilk, cucumber, and brown sugar in a saucepan and cook on low heat. Once mixture begins to boil, remove from heat and immediately add arrowroot cream. This will cause the liquid to thicken noticeably. Add vanilla extract.

Refrigerate mixture until chilled, approximately 2 to 3 hours. Freeze according to your ice cream maker's instructions. In the last few minutes of churning, swirl in peanut butter.

Yield: 1 quart (approximately 600 g)

• One jalapeño plant can produce between 25 to 30 pods and can be picked multiple times during the growing season.

Jalapeño

Jalapeño is an original, super spicy ice cream. It's only for the truly brave! To balance out the spicy flavor, sprinkle some crushed pretzels on top of your scoop.

3 medium-size jalapeño peppers

1 cup (235 ml) soymilk, divided

2 tablespoons (16 g) arrowroot powder

2 cups (470 ml) soy creamer

¾ cup (150 g) sugar

1 tablespoon (15 ml) vanilla extract

In a blender, process jalapeño peppers until smooth. Set aside.

In a small bowl, combine ¼ cup (60 ml) soymilk with arrowroot and set aside.

Mix soy creamer, remaining ¾ cup (175 ml) soymilk, and sugar in a saucepan and cook over low heat. Once mixture begins to boil, remove from heat and immediately add arrowroot cream. This will cause the liquid to thicken noticeably.

Add vanilla extract.

Refrigerate mixture until chilled, approximately 2 to 3 hours. Freeze according to your ice cream maker's instructions. During the last few minutes of churning, add blended jalapeño peppers.

Yield: 1 quart (approximately 600 g)

✳Variation: Raspberry Jalapeño
This combination of sweet and spicy is sure to shock the taste buds.
To make it, simply add ¾ cup (95 g) chopped raspberries
during the last few minutes of churning, at the same time you add
the blended jalapeños.

Carrot Cake

Carrot cake is a great alternative to chocolate or fudge cakes, especially when you're looking for something a bit healthier. Use baby carrots if possible, as their natural sweetness works especially well here.

1 cup (235 ml) soymilk, divided

2 tablespoons (16 g) arrowroot powder

2 cups (470 ml) soy creamer

¾ cup (150 g) sugar

1 tablespoon (15 ml) vanilla extract

1 tablespoon (7 g) ground cinnamon

1 cup (150 g) brown sugar

¼ cup (55 g) non-hydrogenated, non-dairy butter

1½ cups (165 g) grated carrots (peeled if not using baby carrots)

½ cup (75 g) raisins

In a small bowl, combine ¼ cup (60 ml) soymilk with arrowroot and set aside.

Mix soy creamer, remaining ¾ cup (175 ml) soymilk, and sugar in a saucepan and cook over low heat. Once mixture begins to boil, remove from heat and immediately add arrowroot cream. This will cause the liquid to thicken noticeably.

Add vanilla extract and cinnamon. Set aside.

In a small pot over medium heat, combine brown sugar and butter and stir until melted. Add carrots and raisins. Cook on low heat for 5 minutes, or until mixture thickens. Remove from heat and let cool 10 to 15 minutes. Fold into ice cream with a rubber spatula.

Refrigerate mixture until chilled, approximately 2 to 3 hours. Freeze according to your ice cream maker's instructions.

Yield: 1 quart (approximately 600 g)

Tasty Tidbit

- Food historians believe that carrot cake originated from a type of carrot pudding enjoyed during medieval times.

Green Fact

In 2005, the *American Journal of Epidemiology* concluded that people who ate the most meat were atfreezing the greatest risk for heart disease and that a high intake of protein from vegetable sources (e.g., tofu, nuts, and beans) lowers the risk of heart disease by 30 percent.

CHAPTER 7

Aphrodisiacal Flavors

Before settling into my life's work—creating non-dairy ice creams—I fancied myself a romantic. I would spend countless hours wandering the streets of Paris daydreaming about food—desserts specifically—and my love interest of the moment.

A great lover is patient, enthusiastic, and imaginative, I thought. I soon came to realize those are also the traits of a great ice cream maker.

As I took in the sights and sounds of the city of love (which was almost, in and of itself, an aphrodisiac), I thought about how powerful it might be to combine the potency of aphrodisiacal foods with the perfection of ice cream. Ice cream, most frequently eaten after dinner, could serve as a prelude to the rest of the evening, rather than the ending punctuation to a meal.

Regardless of your flavor preference, you can use the recipes in this chapter to heighten your feelings of *amore*. They are perfect for any romantic occasion. But be forewarned: These flavors can sneak up on you. At first, you'll just enjoy the interesting mingling of flavors, but soon, the aphrodisiac will kick in and undoubtedly, you'll feel those sparks fly.

Ginseng

Ginseng root is a popular aphrodisiac. Not only does it contain compounds that increase energy and enhance physical performance, but the shape of the root greatly resembles the human form. Treat yourself—and your partner—to this delicious ice cream.

Tasty Tidbits

- The Chinese name for this sweet licorice-flavored root means "human-shaped root."

- Recent studies have linked ginseng to lowering high blood pressure.

1 cup (235 ml) soymilk, divided

2 tablespoons (16 g) arrowroot powder

2 cups (470 ml) soy creamer

¾ cup (150 g) sugar

1 tablespoon (15 ml) vanilla extract

2 tablespoons (30 ml) ginseng extract

In a small bowl, combine ¼ cup (60 ml) soymilk with arrowroot and set aside.

Mix soy creamer, remaining ¾ cup (175 ml) soymilk, and sugar in a saucepan and cook over low heat. Once mixture begins to boil, remove from heat and immediately add arrowroot cream. This will cause the liquid to thicken noticeably.

Add vanilla and ginseng extracts.

Refrigerate mixture until chilled, approximately 2 to 3 hours. Freeze according to your ice cream maker's instructions.

Yield: 1 quart (approximately 600 g)

SERVING SUGGESTION
Milkshake

Milkshakes are a great way to enjoy any decadent flavor.

3 scoops vegan ice cream

1½ cups (355 ml) soymilk

1 tablespoon (15 ml) vanilla extract

1 teaspoon (7 g) agave nectar

Combine ice cream, soymilk, vanilla, and agave nectar. Blend until smooth.

Yield: Three 8-ounce (250-ml) servings

Jasmine

The sweet aroma of jasmine gives this flower its aphrodisiacal quality. Stimulate your mate with this subtle ice cream, perfect for an evening at home.

1 cup (235 ml) soymilk, divided

2 tablespoons (16 g) arrowroot powder

2 cups (470 ml) soy creamer

½ cup (100 g) sugar

1 tablespoon (15 ml) vanilla extract

2 tablespoons (30 ml) jasmine extract

In a small bowl, combine ¼ cup (60 ml) soymilk with arrowroot and set aside.

Mix soy creamer, remaining ¾ cup (175 ml) soymilk, and sugar in a saucepan and cook over low heat. Once mixture begins to boil, remove from heat and immediately add arrowroot cream. This will cause the liquid to thicken noticeably.

Add vanilla and jasmine extracts.

Refrigerate mixture until chilled, approximately 2 to 3 hours. Freeze according to your ice cream maker's instructions.

Yield: 1 quart (approximately 600 g)

Tasty Tidbits

- The jasmine flower releases its fragrance at night, after the sun has set.

- Jasmine flower buds are more fragrant than jasmine flowers.

Anise

According to the Greeks and the Romans, anise has special aphrodisiac powers. To inspire lust, sprinkle a few of these sweet, aromatic seeds atop ice cream before serving.

1 cup (235 ml) soymilk, divided

2 tablespoons (16 g) arrowroot powder

2 cups (470 ml) soy creamer

½ cup (100 g) sugar

1 tablespoon (15 ml) vanilla extract

2 tablespoons (30 ml) anise extract

In a small bowl, combine ¼ cup (60 ml) soymilk with arrowroot and set aside.

Mix soy creamer, remaining ¾ cup (175 ml) soymilk, and sugar in a saucepan and cook over low heat. Once mixture begins to boil, remove from heat and immediately add arrowroot cream. This will cause the liquid to thicken noticeably.

Add vanilla and anise extracts.

Refrigerate mixture until chilled, approximately 2 to 3 hours. Freeze according to your ice cream maker's instructions.

Yield: 1 quart (approximately 600 g)

Tasty Tidbits

- Anise has been cultivated for more than 4,000 years.

- The Romans used anise as a form of currency.

Rose Water

Since ancient times, roses have symbolized love and beauty. The Greek goddesses Isis and Aphrodite, in particular, considered the rose sacred.

1 cup (235 ml) soymilk, divided

2 tablespoons (16 g) arrowroot powder

2 cups (470 ml) soy creamer

¾ cup (150 g) sugar

1 tablespoon (15 ml) vanilla extract

1 tablespoon (15 ml) rose water

In a small bowl, combine ¼ cup (60 ml) soymilk with arrowroot and set aside.

Mix soy creamer, remaining ¾ cup (175 ml) soymilk, and sugar in a saucepan and cook over low heat. Once mixture begins to boil, remove from heat and immediately add arrowroot cream. This will cause the liquid to thicken noticeably.

Add vanilla extract and rose water.

Refrigerate mixture until chilled, approximately 2 to 3 hours. Freeze according to your ice cream maker's instructions.

Yield: 1 quart (approximately 600 g)

Tasty Tidbit

- Rose water is the liquid remaining after rose petals and water are distilled together to make rose oil. You can make it yourself by combining rose petals and water in a glass jar and letting it sit in the sun for several days.

SERVING SUGGESTION

Gin-Infused Peaches

To make this dessert, you need a mason jar and a flash pickler, a device that removes air from inside a jar (much like a vacuum) and pickles the ingredients within. Alternatively, you can soak the peaches in gin overnight.

2 peaches, peeled, cored, and sliced

½ cup (120 ml) gin (equivalent of 3 shots)

In a mason jar, combine gin and peach slices. Using the flash pickler, remove air from the jar. The peaches are ready to serve immediately.

Yield: 4 servings

Cardamom Rose

Cardamom, an aromatic spice, is a powerful aphrodisiac beneficial in treating impotence and mood. This ice cream, with its cotton candy hue, is sure to lift yours!

1 cup (235 ml) soymilk, divided

2 tablespoons (16 g) arrowroot powder

2 cups (470 ml) soy creamer

¾ cup (150 g) sugar

1 tablespoon (15 ml) vanilla extract

1 tablespoon (6 g) ground cardamom

1 tablespoon (15 ml) rose water

In a small bowl, combine ¼ cup (60 ml) soymilk with arrowroot and set aside.

Mix soy creamer, remaining ¾ cup (175 ml) soymilk, and sugar in a saucepan and cook over low heat. Once mixture begins to boil, remove from heat and immediately add arrowroot cream. This will cause the liquid to thicken noticeably.

Add vanilla extract, cardamom, and rose water.

Refrigerate mixture until chilled, approximately 2 to 3 hours. Freeze according to your ice cream maker's instructions.

Yield: 1 quart (approximately 600 g)

Tasty Tidbit

- Cardamom is native to southwest India and Sri Lanka. It was not grown elsewhere until about 100 years ago, when immigrants moved it to other places. Today, Guatemala is the largest producer of this spice.

Green Fact

When we use grains and legumes more efficiently—as in, for human consumption rather than cattle feed—topsoil automatically becomes more efficient as well.

Pink Pepper Tarragon

This ice cream, which is a soft pink hue, inspires thoughts of love and affection. It's perfect for anniversaries or any other romantic occasion.

1 cup (235 ml) soymilk, divided

2 tablespoons (16 g) arrowroot powder

2 cups (470 ml) soy creamer

¾ cup (150 g) sugar

1 tablespoon (15 ml) vanilla extract

¼ cup (20 g) tarragon spice

¼ cup (25 g) ground Brazilian pink pepper

In a small bowl, combine ¼ cup (60 ml) soymilk with arrowroot and set aside.

Mix soy creamer, remaining ¾ cup (175 ml) soymilk, and sugar in a saucepan and cook over low heat. Once mixture begins to boil, remove from heat and immediately add arrowroot cream. This will cause the liquid to thicken noticeably.

Add vanilla extract, tarragon, and pepper.

Refrigerate mixture until chilled, approximately 2 to 3 hours. Freeze according to your ice cream maker's instructions.

Yield: 1 quart (approximately 600 g)

Tasty Tidbit

- The English word "tarragon" originates from the French word *estragon* or "little dragon," which is derived from the Arabic word *tarkhun*. Some believe the herb was given this name because of its supposed ability to cure the bites of venomous reptiles. Others believe the plant was so named because of its coiled, serpent-like roots.

SERVING SUGGESTION

Jackfruit Sauce

This fruit sauce, with a flavor reminiscent of pineapple, is delectable drizzled on the ice cream above.

½ pound (165 g) frozen jackfruit, thawed

½ cup (120 ml) cold water

¾ cup (175 ml) soymilk

Purée jackfruit in a blender until smooth. Blend in water and soymilk. Serve chilled.

Yield: 3 cups (705 ml)

Lavender

In Tudor times in England, if a maiden wanted to know the identity of her true love, she was told to sip lavender tea and recite a song. In her dreams, her lover would be revealed.

1 cup (235 ml) soymilk, divided

2 tablespoons (16 g) arrowroot powder

2 cups (470 ml) soy creamer

¾ cup (150 g) sugar

1 tablespoon (15 ml) vanilla extract

2 tablespoons (28 ml) lavender extract

In a small bowl, combine ¼ cup (60 ml) soymilk with arrowroot and set aside.

Mix soy creamer, remaining ¾ cup (175 ml) soymilk, and sugar in a saucepan and cook over low heat. Once mixture begins to boil, remove from heat and immediately add arrowroot cream. This will cause the liquid to thicken noticeably.

Add vanilla and lavender extracts.

Refrigerate mixture until chilled, approximately 2 to 3 hours. Freeze according to your ice cream maker's instructions.

Yield: 1 quart (approximately 600 g)

Tasty Tidbit

- Lavender essential oil has antiseptic and anti-inflammatory properties. In World War I, it was used in hospitals as both a healing agent and disinfectant.

SERVING SUGGESTION

Bon Bons

Our subtle Lavender ice cream is the perfect flavor choice for these little treats.

1 pint (approximately 300 g) non-dairy ice cream of choice

18 ounces (505 g) semisweet chocolate

6 tablespoons (84 g) non-hydrogenated, non-dairy butter

6 tablespoons (90 ml) evaporated soymilk

Cover two cookie sheets with waxed paper. Using a melon baller, arrange 40 to 50 mini scoops of ice cream onto one cookie sheet. Place in freezer for 60 minutes.

While ice cream balls freeze, in a double boiler, combine chocolate, butter, and evaporated soymilk over medium heat. Melt mixture until smooth, stirring frequently. Remove from heat.

Remove scoops from freezer, and using spatula and long pronged fork, dip each one into melted chocolate. Coat completely. Transfer to second cookie sheet and immediately place in freezer to harden coating. Serve in muffin cups, if desired.

Yield: 40 to 50 bon bons

Licorice

Chewing on bits of licorice is said to inspire love and lust. Add chopped licorice pieces to this recipe **(pictured at right)** *to enhance the romance factor, or just serve them alongside.*

1 cup (235 ml) soymilk, divided

2 tablespoons (16 g) arrowroot powder

2 cups (470 ml) soy creamer

¾ cup (150 g) sugar

1 tablespoon (15 ml) vanilla extract

2 tablespoons (30 ml) licorice extract

Chopped black licorice, optional

In a small bowl, combine ¼ cup (60 ml) soymilk with arrowroot and set aside.

Mix soy creamer, remaining ¾ cup (175 ml) soymilk, and sugar in a saucepan and cook over low heat. Once mixture begins to boil, remove from heat and immediately add arrowroot cream. This will cause the liquid to thicken noticeably. Add vanilla and licorice extracts.

Refrigerate mixture until chilled, approximately 2 to 3 hours. Freeze according to your ice cream maker's instructions. In the last few minutes of churning, add chopped licorice, if desired.

Yield: 1 quart (approximately 600 g)

Rosemary

Rosemary has a mesmerizing aroma, making it hard for anyone to resist.

1 cup (235 ml) soymilk, divided

2 tablespoons (16 g) arrowroot powder

2 cups (470 ml) soy creamer

¾ cup (150 g) sugar

1 tablespoon (15 ml) vanilla extract

1 tablespoon (15 ml) rosemary extract

In a small bowl, combine ¼ cup (60 ml) soymilk with arrowroot and set aside.

Mix soy creamer, remaining ¾ cup (175 ml) soymilk, and sugar in a saucepan and cook over low heat. Once mixture begins to boil, remove from heat and immediately add arrowroot cream. This will cause the liquid to thicken noticeably. Add vanilla and rosemary extracts.

Refrigerate mixture until chilled, approximately 2 to 3 hours. Freeze according to your ice cream maker's instructions.

Yield: 1 quart (approximately 600 g)

Nutmeg

Nutmeg has been known to awaken the libido and increase sex drive. Give your love life a boost with this delicate, delicious flavor.

1 cup (235 ml) soymilk, divided

2 tablespoons (16 g) arrowroot powder

2 cups (470 ml) soy creamer

¾ cup (150 g) sugar

1 tablespoon (15 ml) vanilla extract

2 tablespoons (14 g) ground nutmeg

In a small bowl, combine ¼ cup (60 ml) soymilk with arrowroot and set aside.

Mix soy creamer, remaining ¾ cup (175 ml) soymilk, and sugar in a saucepan and cook over low heat. Once mixture begins to boil, remove from heat and immediately add arrowroot cream. This will cause the liquid to thicken noticeably.

Add vanilla extract and nutmeg.

Refrigerate mixture until chilled, approximately 2 to 3 hours. Freeze according to your ice cream maker's instructions.

Yield: 1 quart (approximately 600 g)

Tasty Tidbits

- Nutmeg is known as the two-for-one spice because both the nutmeg seed and its lacy covering, known as mace, come from the same plant.

- Nutmeg is one of the oldest spices. It has been cultivated for more than 1,000 years.

- The Caribbean island of Grenada is known as "Nutmeg Isle" because of the large amount of nutmeg it produces.

SERVING SUGGESTION

Caramelized Apples

These apples are a delicious autumn treat and chock-full of flavor.

¼ cup (55 g) non-hydrogenated, non-dairy butter

4 large, tart apples, peeled, cored, and sliced

2 teaspoons (5.4 g) cornstarch

½ cup (120 ml) cold water

¼ cup (28 g) ground nutmeg

Pinch of saffron

In a large skillet or saucepan, melt butter over medium heat; add apples. Cook, stirring constantly, until apples are almost tender, 3 to 4 minutes.

Dissolve cornstarch in water and add mixture to skillet. Stir in nutmeg and saffron, then cook for 2 minutes, stirring occasionally. Remove from heat and serve warm.

Yield: 4 to 6 servings

Fresh Mint Lime

Peppermint has long been considered an aphrodisiac. Its fresh, crisp taste combined with the citrusy tang of lime makes for an irresistible, breath-freshening ice cream.

1 cup (235 ml) soymilk, divided

2 tablespoons (16 g) arrowroot powder

2 cups (470 ml) soy creamer

½ cup (120 ml) lime juice

¾ cup (150 g) sugar

1 tablespoon (15 ml) vanilla extract

1 tablespoon (15 ml) peppermint extract

Mint sprigs, for garnish

In a small bowl, combine ¼ cup (60 ml) soymilk with arrowroot and set aside.

Mix soy creamer, remaining ¾ cup (175 ml) soymilk, lime juice, and sugar in a saucepan and cook over low heat. Once mixture begins to boil, remove from heat and immediately add arrowroot cream. This will cause the liquid to thicken noticeably.

Add vanilla and peppermint extracts.

Refrigerate mixture until chilled, approximately 2 to 3 hours. Freeze according to your ice cream maker's instructions. Garnish with mint sprigs.

Yield: 1 quart (approximately 600 g)

Tasty Tidbit

- Peppermint was one of the earliest herbs discovered. It has been found in Egyptian tombs dating back to 1000 BC, and has been part of the Chinese pharmaco-poeia even longer.

Green Fact

Ninety percent of human exposure to pesticides comes from eating meat. Keep global health issues at bay by following a vegan diet and buying organic produce as often as possible.

Vanilla Brazil Nut

Brazil nuts can raise sexual vibes, attract romance, and improve health and vitality. That means this delectable ice cream promotes mental and physical well-being.

1 cup (235 ml) soymilk, divided

2 tablespoons (16 g) arrowroot powder

2 cups (470 ml) soy creamer

¾ cup (150 g) sugar

1 tablespoon (15 ml) vanilla extract

½ cup (55 g) chopped Brazil nuts

In a small bowl, combine ¼ cup (60 ml) soymilk with arrowroot and set aside.

Mix soy creamer, remaining ¾ cup (175 ml) soymilk, and sugar in a saucepan and cook over low heat. Once mixture begins to boil, remove from heat and immediately add arrowroot cream. This will cause the liquid to thicken noticeably.

Add vanilla extract.

Refrigerate mixture until chilled, approximately 2 to 3 hours. Freeze according to your ice cream maker's instructions. In the last few minutes of churning, add Brazil nuts.

Yield: 1 quart (approximately 600 g)

Tasty Tidbit

- Brazil nuts come in large woody pods resembling coconuts. Each pod holds up to 20 nuts, arranged in sections like a grapefruit.

Green Fact

Vegans and vegetarians tend to weigh less and have less excess body fat than meat-eaters.

Pumpkin and Oats

Pumpkins harmonize a relationship and rehabilitate lost passion. Try serving this ice cream to your loved one after an argument—and don't forget the flowers.

1 cup (235 ml) soymilk, divided

2 tablespoons (16 g) arrowroot powder

2 cups (470 ml) soy creamer

¾ cup (113 g) brown sugar

1 cup (245 g) cooked, mashed pumpkin

2 tablespoons (14 g) pumpkin pie spice

1 tablespoon (15 ml) vanilla extract

½ cup (40 g) oats

In a small bowl, combine ¼ cup (60 ml) soymilk with arrowroot and set aside.

Mix soy creamer, remaining ¾ cup (175 ml) soymilk, brown sugar, pumpkin, and pumpkin spice in a saucepan and cook over low heat. Once mixture begins to boil, remove from heat and immediately add arrowroot cream. This will cause the liquid to thicken noticeably.

Add vanilla extract.

Refrigerate mixture until chilled, approximately 2 to 3 hours. Freeze according to your ice cream maker's instructions. In the last few minutes of churning, add oats.

Yield: 1 quart (approximately 600 g)

Tasty Tidbit

- The name pumpkin originated from the word *pepon*, which is Greek for "large melon."

SERVING SUGGESTION

Oatmeal Cookie Bars

These bars are delicious served warm alongside the ice cream above—or any ice cream for that matter.

½ cup (60 g) all-purpose or whole wheat flour

1½ cups (120 g) rolled oats

½ cup (170 g) agave nectar

½ teaspoon baking soda

½ teaspoon salt

¾ cup (165 g) non-hydrogenated, non-dairy butter, warmed to room temperature

Preheat oven to 350°F (180°C or gas mark 4).

In a large bowl, combine all ingredients until well mixed and evenly press into the bottom of a greased 9 x 13-inch (23 x 33-cm) baking pan. Bake for 15 minutes.

Cool completely before cutting into squares.

Yield: 24 to 28 squares

Sweet Basil

In Italy, basil is a token of love. Give this ice cream creation to your lover as a sign of your affection.

1 cup (235 ml) soymilk, divided

2 tablespoons (16 g) arrowroot powder

3 tablespoons (8 g) chopped, packed fresh sweet basil

2 cups (470 ml) soy creamer

¾ cup (150 g) sugar

1 tablespoon (15 ml) vanilla extract

In a small bowl, combine ¼ cup (60 ml) soymilk with arrowroot and set aside.

In a food processor, blend remaining ¾ cup (175 ml) soymilk and basil until smooth. Set aside.

Mix soy creamer, basil-milk blend, and sugar in a saucepan and cook over low heat. Once mixture begins to boil, remove from heat and immediately add arrowroot cream. This will cause the liquid to thicken noticeably.

Add vanilla extract.

Refrigerate mixture until chilled, approximately 2 to 3 hours. Freeze according to your ice cream maker's instructions.

Yield: 1 quart (approximately 600 g)

✻Variations: Cinnamon, Lemon, or Lime Basil

For additional flavor combinations, try adding 3 tablespoons (21 g) ground cinnamon or 3 tablespoons (45 ml) lemon or lime juice. Put in the special ingredient when you add the vanilla extract.

Tasty Tidbit

- Basil is purported to have many medicinal proprties, including the ability to soothe stomach pain, headaches, and anxiety.

Tasty Tidbit

- Thai chile peppers are also called bird peppers.

Thai Chile

It has been said that chile pepper acts as an aphrodisiac because of the physiological responses it causes—most notably, an increase in heart rate. To spice up your next date, add this flavorful ice cream to your menu.

3½ medium-size Thai chile peppers, chopped, divided

1 cup (235 ml) soymilk, divided

2 tablespoons (16 g) arrowroot powder

2 cups (470 ml) soy creamer

¾ cup (150 g) sugar

1 tablespoon (15 ml) vanilla extract

In a blender, process 3 chile peppers until smooth.

In a small bowl, combine ¼ cup (60 ml) soymilk with arrowroot and set aside.

Mix soy creamer, remaining ¾ cup (175 ml) soymilk, puréed chile peppers, and sugar in a saucepan and cook over low heat. Once mixture begins to boil, remove from heat and immediately add arrowroot cream. This will cause the liquid to thicken noticeably.

Add vanilla extract.

Refrigerate mixture until chilled, approximately 2 to 3 hours. Freeze according to your ice cream maker's instructions. In the last few minutes of churning, add additional ½ chopped chile pepper, if desired.

Yield: 1 quart (approximately 600 g)

Green Fact

Unsanitary, cramped conditions at factory farms increase the risk of animal-borne diseases such as E. coli, salmonella, and avian influenza. Cutting meat out of your diet places you at reduced risk for contracting these dangerous pathogens.

Coconut Lemongrass

According to legend, lemongrass gives you the ability to attract the object of your desire. To enhance lust, sprinkle shreds of coconut atop this aphrodisiac ice cream.

3½ cups (825 ml) coconut milk, divided

2 tablespoons (16 g) arrowroot powder

¾ cup (150 g) sugar

1 tablespoon (15 ml) vanilla extract

1½ teaspoons (8 ml) lemongrass extract

In a small bowl, combine ¼ cup (60 ml) coconut milk with arrowroot and set aside.

Mix remaining 3¼ cups (765 ml) coconut milk and sugar in a saucepan, and cook over low heat. Once mixture begins to boil, remove from heat and immediately add arrowroot cream. This will cause the liquid to thicken noticeably.

Stir in vanilla and lemongrass extracts.

Refrigerate mixture until chilled, approximately 2 to 3 hours. Freeze according to your ice cream maker's instructions.

Yield: 1 quart (approximately 600 g)

Tasty Tidbit

- Lemongrass has many medicinal purposes. It aids in the management of gastrointestinal and nervous system disorders, treats fevers, and works as an analgesic.

SERVING SUGGESTION

Peanut Butter Ice Cream Sandwiches

These peanut butter cookie sandwiches will be a hit no matter which ice cream flavor you choose to pair them with!

1¼ cups (155 g) all-purpose flour, sifted or stirred before measuring

½ teaspoon salt

1 teaspoon (4.6 g) baking powder

½ cup (100 g) vegan shortening

½ cup (130 g) peanut butter

½ cup (170 g) agave nectar

½ teaspoon vanilla extract

1 tablespoon (12 g) ground flaxseed

3 tablespoons (45 ml) water

1 pint (approximately 300 g) vegan ice cream of choice, softened

Preheat oven to 375°F (190°C or gas mark 5). Sift together flour, salt, and baking powder and set aside.

Cream shortening, peanut butter, and agave nectar. Beat in vanilla, flaxseed, and water. Stir in flour mixture, blending well.

Shape dough into ¾-inch (2-cm) balls and place on greased baking sheets. Flatten each cookie with the tines of a fork (dip fork in flour periodically to keep it from sticking to dough).

Bake 10 to 12 minutes.

Once cookies are cooled, spread a 1-inch (2.5-cm) layer of softened ice cream onto one cookie and top with a second cookie. Repeat with remaining cookies and freeze for an additional 15 to 20 minutes to allow sandwiches to firm up.

Yield: 15 to 20 ice cream sandwiches

Chocolate Martini Sorbet

*This spiked chocolate sorbet (**pictured at right**) makes for a smooth finish to any meal or special occasion.*

½ cup (120 g) agave nectar

2 teaspoons (10 ml) gin

2 teaspoons (10 ml) vermouth

2 teaspoons (10 ml) chocolate liqueur

1 quart (940 ml) water

Combine all ingredients. Place mixture in ice cream maker and freeze according to instructions.

Yield: 1 quart (approximately 600 g)

> ✳Variations: Apple, Pear, or Blueberry Martini
> To make any of these tasty variations, use 1 ½ tablespoons (23 ml) apple, pear, or blueberry juice instead of chocolate liqueur. Serve with fresh fruit and a sprinkle of brown sugar.

Mojito Sorbet

A Mojito is a Cuban cocktail made of light rum, mint, lime, and sugar. Here we substitute agave nectar for the sugar. This sorbet is best served on a hot summer night.

½ cup (170 g) agave nectar

3 fresh mint sprigs

1½ tablespoons (23 ml) lime juice

2 tablespoons (28 ml) light rum

1 quart (940 ml) water

Combine all ingredients. Place mixture in ice cream maker and freeze according to instructions.

Yield: 1 quart (approximately 600 g)

> ✳Variation: Orange Mojito
> For a bright, orangey citrus burst, substitute 1 ½ tablespoons (23 ml) orange juice for the lime juice.

Champagne Sorbet

This sorbet calls for a celebration! For delicate texture and exquisite taste, make sure to use high-quality champagne.

½ cup (170 g) agave nectar

2 tablespoons (28 ml) champagne

1 quart (940 ml) water

Combine all ingredients. Place mixture in ice cream maker and freeze according to instructions.

Yield: 1 quart (approximately 600 g)

✱Variation: Pomegranate Champagne Sorbet
To give this sorbet a fresh, sweet taste, add 1 ½ tablespoons (23 ml) pomegranate juice.

SERVING SUGGESTION
Chocolate-Covered Strawberries

Nothing tops an evening like these chocolate-covered delicacies.

2 cups (350 g) vegan chocolate chips

2 tablespoons (28 g) non-hydrogenated, non-dairy butter

10 to 15 fresh strawberries, with leaves

Cover a baking pan with waxed paper and set aside.

In a double boiler, melt chocolate and butter, stirring until smooth. Dip strawberries into chocolate mixture, one at a time, then lay on waxed paper to dry.

Harden in refrigerator for at least 30 minutes before serving.

Yield: 10 to 15 Strawberries

CHAPTER 8

Ice Cream Vessels and Sauces

"Life is uncertain. Eat dessert first."

—Ernestine Ulmer, American writer

Our frozen desserts are incredible by themselves, but to make them truly irresistible, why not add toppings? And while we're at it, why not turn the vessel that holds the frozen goodness into its own satisfying treat?

We could write an entire book about toppings and creative ways to present our ice cream, but for the sake of space, we've narrowed down this topic to sauces and vessels that match the dessert recipes we've already presented.

Have fun with these suggestions: Mix and match, create your own, even experiment with edible spoons and out-of-this-world sundaes. Most importantly, have fun and enjoy our ice cream!

Sugar Cones

We made these classics into vegan treats anyone will enjoy. Don't forget to pinch the tip so ice cream won't drip out the bottom.

¼ cup (60 ml) water

2 tablespoons (28 ml) vegetable oil

¼ cup (55 g) baking powder

½ cup (100 g) organic cane sugar (similar to granulated sugar)

¼ cup (55 g) non-dairy, non-hydrogenated butter, melted and cooled

3 tablespoons (45 ml) soymilk

½ teaspoon vanilla extract

⅓ cup (42 g) all-purpose flour

⅛ teaspoon salt

In a medium-size bowl, combine water, oil, baking powder, and sugar. Mix well, then whisk in melted butter, milk, and vanilla extract. Add flour and salt, and continue to whisk until batter is thin and smooth.

Heat a medium-size sauté pan until hot. Reduce heat to medium-low and lightly brush pan with vegetable oil. Ladle ¼ cup (approximately 60 ml) batter onto pan, immediately tilting so batter forms a 5-inch (13-cm) circle. Cook until golden brown. Using a metal spatula, flip over and cook until pancake turns golden brown on other side.

Remove from heat. While still hot, roll crepe into a cone shape, squeezing tip to seal. Cool completely.

Yield: 30 cones

---

*Variation: Chocolate-Dipped Sugar Cone

To spice up the traditional sugar cone, melt 1½ cups (265 g) vegan chocolate chips, stirring until smooth. Dip top of cooled cone into chocolate and place on waxed paper to harden. For some color, dip in vegan rainbow sprinkles before allowing chocolate to harden.

Hot Fudge

*Who doesn't love a hot fudge sundae? This delicious topper **(pictured at right)** is delightful drizzled over a frosty dish of ice cream.*

2 cups (400 g) organic cane
  sugar (similar to granulated sugar)

1 cup (150 g) brown sugar

1 cup (80 g) cocoa powder

½ teaspoon salt

¼ cup (30 g) all-purpose flour

¼ cup (55 g) non-hydrogenated,
  non-dairy butter

1½ cups (355 ml) water

½ teaspoon vanilla extract

Mix dry ingredients, through flour, in a large saucepan. Add butter and water.

Over low heat, bring mixture to a boil and cook for 10 minutes. Remove from heat, then add vanilla and stir. Serve immediately, or let sit for a few minutes to slightly thicken.

Yield: 2 cups (475 ml)

Butterscotch

This candy sauce is a vegan take on a sweet-tooth favorite. It goes great with any of our ice creams.

1 cup (150 g) brown sugar

½ cup (120 ml) soy creamer

2¼ tablespoons (30 g) non-hydrogenated, non-dairy butter

2 tablespoons (30 ml) maple syrup

In a medium-size saucepan, combine all ingredients. Bring to a boil on medium heat, stirring often.

Once mixture begins to boil, remove from heat, cool slightly, and serve.

Yield: 2 cups (475 ml)

What's in a Name?

Here, we explain some common food-prep methods, so you'll never again confuse "fondant" with "foam."

Compote: A stew-like dish made by gently poaching fresh or dried fruit in sweet syrup or liqueur. It is often seasoned with spices such as cloves or cinnamon.

Confit: A generic term to describe fruits and vegetables that have been slow-cooked in their own juices and infused with sugar to become jam-like sauces or spreads.

Consommé: A rich, flavorful broth clarified so it is transparent.

Coulis: A smooth sauce made from puréed fruits or vegetables that have been strained of seeds and peels.

Foam: A dessert sauce made with milk, brown sugar, and chocolate or coffee. It is heated, chilled, and then placed into a siphon to produce a stiff substance to top desserts.

Fondant: A sweet, thick icing made from a mixture of sugar, water, syrup, and sometimes, cream of tartar. It is cooked and then kneaded to a smooth, soft consistency to be spread over cakes and other sweets.

Tartar: A white powder that often gives candy and fruit a creamy texture.

Port Reduction: A type of sauce usually made of Port wine, stock, and a variety of vegetables, fruits, and herbs. It is cooked over high heat until it thickens and reduces.

Ratatouille: A stew often made with eggplant, tomatoes, peppers, and a variety of seasonings. It can be made into a dessert topping by using fruit instead.

Caramel Sauce

It's easy to confuse caramel and butterscotch. The two are similar in appearance and flavor, but they differ in one significant way: the type of sugar in the recipe. Conduct a taste test and decide for yourself whether you like butterscotch, caramel—or both!

1 cup (200 g) sugar

6 tablespoons (84 g) non-hydrogenated, non-dairy butter

½ cup (120 ml) soy creamer

In a thick-bottomed 2- or 3-quart (1.9- or 2.8-L) saucepan, heat sugar on medium heat, whisking as it melts. When sugar reaches a boil, stop stirring.

Once sugar melts completely, add butter and whisk until melted.

Remove from heat and slowly incorporate creamer. Mixture should foam or bubble considerably. Whisk until caramel is smooth. Let cool slightly before serving.

Pour unused or leftover caramel into a jar and let cool completely. Store in refrigerator for up to 2 weeks. Warm before serving.

Yield: 2 cups (475 ml)

Peanut Butter Sauce

Peanut butter burns easily, so pay attention when preparing this sauce. Its smooth, nut flavor works great on any of our ice creams.

1 cup (200 g) sugar

½ cup (120 ml) water

½ teaspoon salt

⅔ cup (227 g) agave nectar

1 cup (260 g) peanut butter

In a small saucepan, combine sugar, water, salt, and agave nectar and bring to a boil over low heat.

Boil for 1 minute, then turn off heat and let cool for 2 to 3 minutes.

While mixture is cooling, whip peanut butter. Incorporate it into mixture with a wire whip. Serve warm.

Store in refrigerator for up to 2 weeks. Heat before serving.

Yield: 2 cups (475 ml)

- Berries freeze exceptionally well and are a great treat to have on hand during off-season months. To freeze, simply spread berries on a baking sheet and place in the freezer. Once frozen, transfer berries to a freezer bag or container and return to freezer.

Very Berry Sauce

For a special treat, whip up a batch of your favorite vegan waffles and top with some ice cream and this fruity sauce. For optimal taste, make this recipe during summertime, which is peak berry season.

2 cups (290 g) blueberries, raspberries, or sliced strawberries (or a combination of all three)

½ cup (100 g) sugar

2 teaspoons (10 g) agave nectar

Juice of ½ lemon

Pinch of salt

In a medium-size saucepan, combine all ingredients.

On medium heat, stir mixture gently for 10 minutes, or until sugar dissolves and berries are soft. Remove from heat and cool.

Yield: 2 cups (475 ml)

Green Fact

Nearly one-third of the earth's land is used to raise and feed livestock.

CHAPTER 9

Ice Cream Sides and Desserts

You are probably familiar with household staples such as flour, vegetable oil, baking soda, salt, and hopefully by now, soymilk. Though these may appear to be simple baking ingredients, the interactions caused by their various chemical components make for pretty complex science.

For instance, baking soda is a leavening agent, which, when added to dough and heated above 122°F (50°C), causes it to rise. That means if you happen to be an absent-minded baker, forgetting to include baking soda in a recipe will result in hard, small dough—and definitely not something you'll want to eat!

For this reason, many people consider baking—especially vegan baking—a difficult and fickle task. But following our tips and guidance, these recipes will be, dare we say it, a piece of cake.

If you're a beginner, first try the easier recipes such as cookies, brownies, and cupcakes. Practice makes perfect and a good understanding of the basics will only help you in the long run. Don't be afraid to experiment and as always, have fun!

Chocolate Fudge Brownies

These gooey, fudgy brownies are delicious served with ice cream or in it! To make them suitable for the latter option, wrap the brownies in plastic, freeze for 4 to 5 hours, then cut them into bite-size pieces. Add to ice cream in the last few minutes of churning.

2 cups (250 g) all-purpose flour

2 cups (400 g) organic cane sugar (similar to granulated sugar)

¾ cup (60 g) unsweetened cocoa powder

1 teaspoon (4.6 g) baking powder

1 teaspoon (6 g) salt

½ cup (120 ml) water

½ cup (120 ml) soymilk

¼ cup (59 ml) vegetable oil

1 teaspoon (5 ml) vanilla extract

½ cup (60 g) chopped walnuts, optional

Preheat oven to 350°F (180°C or gas mark 4). Grease 9 x 13-inch (23 x 33-cm) baking pan.

In a large bowl, combine flour, sugar, cocoa powder, baking powder, and salt and stir. Add water, soymilk, vegetable oil, and vanilla extract. Mix until well blended.

Evenly spread batter into pan and sprinkle with nuts, if desired. Bake for 25 to 30 minutes. Let cool, then cut into squares.

Yield: 24 to 28 brownies

✳Variation: Peanut Butter Brownies

To make a peanut butter variety of the Chocolate Fudge Brownies, use ¾ cup (175 ml) water instead of ½ cup (120 ml) and add ½ cup (130 g) peanut butter after the vanilla extract.

✳Variation: Chocolate Chip Brownies with Chocolate Icing

For more chocolatey goodness, add 1 cup (175 g) vegan chocolate chips to the batter after blending all other ingredients. To make chocolate icing, combine 1 cup (200 g) sugar, 6 tablespoons (48 g) cornstarch, ½ teaspoon salt, and ¼ cup (20 g) cocoa powder. Whisk in ½ cup (120 ml) water and ¼ cup (60 ml) soymilk and cook over medium heat until boiling. Continue boiling for 1 to 2 minutes. Remove from heat and stir in 2 tablespoons (28 ml) vegetable oil and 1 tablespoon (15 ml) vanilla extract. Cool and spread onto brownies.

Blondies

A "backwards brownie" of sorts, blondies are a rich, decadent treat. Serve a scoop of Peanut Butter ice cream (page 51) alongside one of these and you'll be in seventh heaven.

Non-hydrogenated, non-dairy butter, for greasing

1¼ cups (155 g) flour, plus more for dusting

¾ teaspoon baking soda

½ teaspoon salt

6 ounces (170 g) vanilla soy yogurt

¼ cup (60 ml) canola oil

1 tablespoon (15 ml) vanilla

2 tablespoons (30 ml) molasses

1 cup (200 g) sugar

¾ cup (135 g) chocolate chips

Preheat oven to 350°F (180°C or gas mark 4) and lightly butter and flour an 8 x 8-inch (20 x 20-cm) pan.

In a medium bowl, mix flour, baking soda, and salt. Set aside.

In a large bowl, combine yogurt, oil, vanilla, and molasses. Stir until blended, then add sugar and mix until well combined.

Slowly fold dry ingredients into the wet ingredients, mixing until just combined. Stir in chocolate chips.

Pour batter into prepared pan and bake for 30 minutes. Allow to cool, then cut into squares and serve.

Yield: 16 blondies

Green Fact

One-thousand species become extinct each year because of the destruction of the tropical rainforest.

Chocolate Chip Biscotti

These twice-baked goodies are delicious alongside a steaming mug of hot chocolate on a blustery winter afternoon or with our decadent Coffee ice cream (page 58).

3 tablespoons (23 g) ground flaxseed

9 Tablespoons (135 ml) water

1 teaspoon (5 ml) vanilla extract

½ teaspoon almond extract

2 cups (250 g) all-purpose flour

⅜ cup (90 g) agave nectar

1 teaspoon (4.6 g) baking powder

⅛ teaspoon salt

1 cup (175 g) vegan chocolate chips

Preheat oven to 350°F (180°C or gas mark 4) and line a baking sheet with parchment paper.

In a small bowl, lightly beat ground flaxseed, water, and vanilla and almond extracts until slightly frothy and gelatinous.

In the bowl of an electric mixer, combine flour, agave nectar, baking powder, and salt. Beat for 30 seconds, or until thoroughly blended.

Gradually add flaxseed mixture and beat until dough forms. Add chocolate chips about halfway through the process.

Transfer dough to a lightly floured surface and divide in half. Shape each half into a log about 10-inches (25-cm) long and 2-inches (5-cm) wide. Slide logs onto prepared baking sheet, spacing them about 3 inches (7.5 cm) apart. Bake until slightly firm, 22 to 25 minutes.

Cool for 5 minutes. Reduce oven to 300°F (150°C or gas mark 2).

Using a serrated knife, cut biscotti diagonally into 1-inch (2.5-cm) thick slices. Arrange evenly on baking sheet. Bake 10 minutes, turn over, and bake another 10 minutes or until firm to the touch. Remove from oven and let cool completely.

Yield: 40 biscotti

Tasty Tidbit

- The name "biscotti" derives from the Italian words *bis*, meaning "twice" and *cotto*, meaning "baked or cooked."

Classic Chocolate Chip Cookies

Who can resist a homemade chocolate chip cookie straight from the oven? This recipe offers a vegan twist on a classic. Delicious!

2 cups plus 2 tablespoons (265 g) all-purpose flour

½ teaspoon sea salt

½ teaspoon baking soda

12 tablespoons (168 g) non-hydrogenated, non-dairy butter, softened

1 cup (225 g) light brown sugar, packed

½ cup (100 g) granulated sugar or evaporated cane juice

1½ teaspoons Ener-G egg replacer, whisked together with 2 tablespoons (28 ml) of water, for the equivalent of one egg

2 teaspoons (10 ml) vanilla extract

1 to 1½ cups (175 to 260 g) vegan chocolate chips

Preheat oven to 350°F (180°C or gas mark 4).

Mix flour, salt, and baking soda in medium-size bowl.

Using an electric mixer, cream together butter and sugars. Add Ener-G egg mixture and vanilla, and mix until well combined.

Incorporate dry ingredients into wet, being careful not to over mix (by hand is preferable). Stir in chocolate chips.

Portion cookies onto a parchment paper-lined cookie sheet using a #40 cookie scoop or rounded tablespoon. For larger, bakery-size cookies, use a small measuring cup, such as ¼ cup. Flatten slightly using any flat-bottomed surface (such as a damp glass).

Bake 8 to 10 minutes. Cool on sheet for several minutes before transferring to wire rack to cool completely.

Yield: 25 traditional-size or 16 bakery-style cookies

> *Variation: Chocolate Chocolate Chip Cookies
> To make even richer melt-in-your-mouth cookies, throw in ⅔ cup (55 g) cocoa powder when you add the flour. You'll certainly impress your friends—especially the chocolate lovers.

Sugar Cookies with Icing and Sprinkles

Sweet, crispy sugar cookies make a great treat all year round. Shape and decorate them for any holiday season! Hint: For a burst of color, add a few drops of food coloring to the icing.

For Cookies:

2 tablespoons (25 g) organic cane sugar (similar to granulated sugar)

2 tablespoons (14 g) ground cinnamon

½ cup (110 g) plus 2 tablespoons (28 g) non-hydrogenated, non-dairy butter

½ cup (100 g) sugar

1 tablespoon (15 ml) vanilla extract

1½ cups (185 g) all-purpose flour

½ teaspoon baking soda

½ teaspoon salt

¼ cup (60 ml) soymilk

For Icing:

2 cups (240 g) confectioners' sugar

2⅔ tablespoons (38 ml) soymilk

2 teaspoons (10 ml) corn syrup

½ teaspoon vanilla extract

Food coloring, optional

Vegan sprinkles, optional

Tasty Tidbit

- Most non-vegan sprinkles contain beeswax or "confectioners' glaze," which contains insect-derived ingredients, so it's important to read labels carefully.

To make cookies: Preheat oven to 350°F (180°C or gas mark 4).

In a small bowl, combine organic cane sugar and cinnamon and set aside.

With a mixer, blend butter and ½ cup (100 g) regular sugar until fluffy. Add vanilla extract. Add remaining dry ingredients, stir, then add soymilk. Mix well.

Form balls with dough and roll them in sugar-cinnamon mixture. Place on ungreased cookie sheet and bake for 10 to 12 minutes, until golden.

To make icing: Combine confectioners' sugar and soymilk in a medium-size bowl and stir until smooth. Beat in corn syrup and vanilla extract.

Add food coloring, if desired.

Spread icing (and sprinkles, if desired) onto cookies and allow to harden overnight on waxed paper.

Yield: 24 cookies

Oatmeal Raisin Cookies

These wholesome cookies are served best with a tall glass of chocolate soymilk.

¾ cup (165 g) non-hydrogenated, non-dairy butter, warmed to room temperature

½ cup (100 g) sugar

1 cup (225 g) packed brown sugar

1 teaspoon (5 ml) vanilla extract

½ cup (120 ml) soymilk

1 cup (125 g) all-purpose flour

½ teaspoon baking soda

½ teaspoon salt

1 teaspoon (2.3 g) cinnamon

½ cup (60 g) ground flaxseed

1 cup (145 g) raisins

3 cups (240 g) rolled oats

Preheat oven to 350°F (180°C or gas mark 4).

In a medium-size bowl, combine butter, sugar, brown sugar, and vanilla extract until light and fluffy. Add soymilk and mix well.

Add flour, baking soda, salt, cinnamon, and flaxseed and stir until well mixed. Add raisins and oats and continue stirring until batter becomes thick.

Drop 3-inch (7.5-cm) balls of dough onto ungreased baking sheet and flatten slightly. Bake for 10 to 12 minutes, then place cookies on a cooling rack.

Yield: 24 cookies

Green Fact

Raising livestock for human consumption greatly adds to the release of methane into the atmosphere, which has 23 times the global warming potential of carbon dioxide.

Mini Sandwich Cookies

These cookies are delicate and mild with a wonderful burst of chocolate.

⅓ cup (80 ml) soymilk

¾ cup (150 g) sugar

½ cup (120 ml) vegetable oil

2 teaspoons (10 ml) vanilla
extract

Pinch lemon zest

2 cups (250 g) all-purpose flour

2 tablespoons (16 g) cornstarch

1 teaspoon (4.6 g) baking powder

¼ teaspoon salt

½ cup (90 g) vegan chocolate chips

Preheat oven to 350 °F (180 °C or gas mark 4).Grease two cookie sheets, then set aside.

In a large mixing bowl, combine milk, sugar, oil, vanilla, and lemon zest and mix well. Add flour, cornstarch, baking powder, and salt, and mix well until substance becomes dough-like.

Flour hands and surface area, then roll dough into 2-inch (5-cm) long, thin logs. Be sure to flour your hands before molding each cookie or dough will stick.

Place dough logs on cookie sheet and bake 15 minutes, until cookies are firm and edges are browned. Set aside to cool.

In a small saucepan, melt chocolate chips over medium heat, stirring until smooth.

Once cookies have cooled, spoon melted chocolate onto one cookie, then place another cookie on top, forming a sandwich. Place on a large plate and refrigerate to set.

Yield: 16 cookie sandwiches

Boston Cream Pie

This rich creamy dessert—actually a cake, not a pie—looks as good as it tastes. It's sure to impress even the most finicky of eaters!

For Cake:

2 cups (250 g) all-purpose flour

1 teaspoon (4.6 g) baking powder

1 teaspoon (4.6 g) baking soda

½ teaspoon salt

1¼ cups (250 g) sugar

½ cup (120 ml) vegetable oil

½ cup (115 g) soy yogurt

1½ cups (355 ml) soymilk

2 teaspoons (10 ml) vanilla extract

For Cream Filling:

⅓ cup (65 g) sugar

Pinch of salt

2 tablespoons (16 g) cornstarch

1½ cups (355 ml) vanilla soymilk

1 tablespoon (14 g) margarine

1 teaspoon (5 ml) vanilla extract

For Chocolate Sauce:

¼ cup (55 g) non-hydrogenated, non-dairy butter

¼ cup (60 ml) chocolate soymilk

⅓ cup (60 g) vegan chocolate chips

To make cake: Preheat oven to 350°F (180°C or gas mark 4). Grease and flour two 9-inch (23-cm) round cake pans and line with parchment paper. Set aside.

In a large bowl, combine flour, baking powder, baking soda, and salt. Mix and set aside.

In another large bowl, combine sugar with oil and stir until incorporated. Add soy yogurt, soymilk, and vanilla extract and mix until creamy.

Combine wet and dry ingredients until mixture becomes a batter-like consistency. Divide evenly into cake pans. Bake for 20 to 25 minutes, then set aside to cool.

To make cream filling: In a medium-size saucepan, combine sugar, salt, cornstarch, and soymilk. Over medium heat, bring to a boil, whisking constantly. Lower to a simmer and continue to whisk for 5 minutes, or until thick. Remove from heat.

Add margarine and vanilla. Pour mixture into a bowl and let cool, stirring every few minutes.

To make chocolate sauce: In a small saucepan over medium heat, melt butter. Stirring constantly, add soymilk. Remove from heat and add chocolate chips. Whisk until chocolate melts, then let cool for several minutes.

Place one cake on a platter and spread cream filling on top. Place other cake on top and cover with chocolate sauce. Refrigerate for at least 45 minutes before serving.

Yield: One 9-inch (23-cm) double-layer cake, 8 to 10 slices

Tasty Tidbit

- Madeleines are similar in flavor to pound cake, but with a much lighter texture.

French Madeleines

A traditional French Madeleine has a distinct and exact texture. These cake-like cookies should be light, slightly crisp, and golden brown. To achieve this, we recommend using a brand-name egg replacer, such as Ener-G. However, feel free to experiment with other egg substitutes.

½ cup (110 g) non-hydrogenated, non-dairy butter

¼ cup (30 g) all-purpose flour

½ cup (60 g) almond flour

1½ teaspoons (9 g) salt

½ cup (100 g) plus 2 tablespoons (25 g) sugar

3 Ener-G eggs (or other egg substitute)

¾ teaspoon (4 ml) lemon juice

2 tablespoons (12 g) finely grated lemon zest

Preheat oven to 375°F (190°C or gas mark 5).

In a small bowl, melt butter and let cool. Set aside.

In a medium-size bowl, combine two flours and salt. Add sugar and egg replacement and beat until frothy.

Add lemon juice and zest, then slowly add melted butter. Stir until incorporated.

Lightly grease and flour a Madeleine pan (which looks like a muffin tin, but has spaces meant specifically for this type of cookie). Fill each shell about ⅔ full with batter. Bake for 15 to 20 minutes, or until crisp and brown around the edges.

Yield: 24 cookies

Green Fact

Albert Einstein once said, "Nothing will benefit human health and increase the chances of survival of life on earth as much as the evolution to a vegetarian diet."

Twinkies

This playful, cream-filled treat is both exciting to bake and fun to eat! It'll be a hit at every child's birthday party. For best results, make in the traditional twinkie pan. Alternatively, use muffin tins.

For Batter:

1 cup (125 g) all-purpose flour

¾ teaspoon baking soda

½ teaspoon baking powder

¼ teaspoon salt

1 cup (235 ml) soymilk

1 teaspoon (5 ml) apple cider vinegar

¾ cup (150 g) sugar

⅓ cup (80 ml) canola oil

2 teaspoons (10 ml) vanilla extract

For Cream Filling:

½ cup (110 g) non-hydrogenated, non-dairy butter

1 cup (100 g) confectioners' sugar

1 teaspoon (5 ml) vanilla extract

2 tablespoons (16 g) barley malt powder (a natural sweetener derived from barley)

To make batter: Preheat oven to 350°F (180°C or gas mark 4).

In a large bowl, combine flour, baking soda, baking powder, and salt. Set aside.

In another large bowl, combine soymilk and vinegar; whisk. Wait for mixture to curdle, then add sugar, oil, and vanilla. Beat until foamy. Pour mixture into dry ingredients and beat until smooth.

Grease pan with vegan non-stick spray and pour batter into cups until ¼ full. Bake for 15 minutes.

To make filling: Combine butter and confectioners' sugar in a medium-size bowl and beat until light and fluffy. Add vanilla and malt powder and beat until incorporated.

Using a pastry bag, poke three holes into bottom of each baked pastry and inject 1 tablespoon (15 g) cream filling into each hole.

Yield: 16 twinkies

Cupcakes

Served alongside a scoop of ice cream, these cupcakes are a real treat.

1 tablespoon (15 ml) apple cider vinegar

1½ cups (355 ml) soymilk

2 cups plus 2 tablespoons (265 g) all-purpose flour

1 cup plus 2 tablespoons (225 g) sugar

½ teaspoon baking powder

½ teaspoon baking soda

½ teaspoon salt

½ cup (120 ml) vegetable oil

1 tablespoon (15 ml) vanilla extract

Preheat oven to 350°F (180°C or gas mark 4). Line muffin pan with cupcake liners and set aside.

In a small bowl, combine vinegar and soymilk. Stir well. Set aside to curdle.

In a large bowl, combine flour, sugar, baking powder, baking soda, and salt.

In another bowl, combine soymilk mixture, oil, and vanilla extract. Add to dry ingredients and beat until smooth.

Fill each cupcake liner ⅔ full of batter. Bake for 15 to 20 minutes, until a toothpick comes out clean. Let cupcakes cool before frosting.

Yield: 12 cupcakes

✳Variations: Ginger, Lemon, or Chocolate Cupcakes

• **For Ginger Cupcakes**, add in 1 tablespoon (5.5 g) ground ginger and 1¼ cups (125 g) finely chopped crystallized ginger to dry ingredients.

• **For Lemon Cupcakes**, add 2½ teaspoons (5 g) lemon zest to dry-ingredient mix and 2 tablespoons (28 ml) lemon juice to wet ingredients.

• **For Chocolate Cupcakes**, add ¾ cup (60 g) cocoa powder to dry ingredients and ¾ cup (130 g) vegan chocolate chips to final batter.

Italian White Cream Cake

This smooth, white-chocolate cake is an unforgettable finish to any meal. Serve with a dish of decadent ice cream or sorbet.

For White Chocolate:

¼ cup (55 g) cocoa butter

1 teaspoon (5 ml) vanilla extract

⅓ cup (40 g) confectioners' sugar

½ teaspoon soymilk powder

Pinch of salt

For Cake:

3 cups (375 g) all-purpose flour, sifted

2 teaspoons (9.2 g) baking powder

½ teaspoon salt

½ cup (110 g) non-hydrogenated, non-dairy butter, warmed to room temperature

1¼ cups (250 g) sugar

1 cup plus 2 tablespoons (265 ml) soymilk

1 teaspoon (5 ml) vanilla extract

To make white chocolate: Microwave cocoa butter for 1 to 2 minutes, until melted. Quickly stir in remaining ingredients, blending until smooth. Set aside.

To make batter: Preheat oven to 350°F (180°C or gas mark 4). Butter and flour two 9-inch (23-cm) round cake pans.

In a medium-size bowl, combine flour, baking powder, and salt. Stir and set aside.

In a large bowl, combine butter and sugar and beat until light and fluffy. Add soymilk, vanilla, and white chocolate mixture and beat until combined. Slowly add dry ingredients and stir until smooth.

Pour batter into prepared pans and bake for 25 to 30 minutes, or until top is golden.

Yield: Two 9-inch (23-cm) round cakes, or 16 slices

Chocolate Chip Ice Cream Cake

This cake is perfect for any occasion! Use a creative ice cream flavor such as Green Tea (page 122) or Brown Sugar Caramel (page 167) to give the dessert a unique, personal touch.

3 cups (375 g) all-purpose flour

2 cups (400 g) sugar

½ cup (40 g) cocoa powder

2 teaspoons (9.2 g) baking soda

2 teaspoons (10 ml) vanilla extract

2 teaspoons (10 ml) distilled vinegar

½ cup (120 ml) vegetable oil

2 cups (470 ml) water

1 cup (175 g) vegan chocolate chips

1 quart (approximately 600 g) non-dairy ice cream

Preheat oven to 350°F (180°C or gas mark 4).

Grease and flour two 9-inch (23-cm) round cake pans and set aside.

In a medium-size bowl, combine flour, sugar, cocoa powder, and baking soda. Pour in vanilla, vinegar, oil, and water and stir well. Fold in chocolate chips. Pour mixture into cake pans, dividing evenly. Bake for 30 to 35 minutes. Allow cakes to cool before removing from pans.

Soften ice cream by microwaving for 10 seconds. Place one cake on a serving platter and spread on ice cream. Carefully place other cake on top of ice cream.

Place cake, uncovered, in freezer for 3 to 4 hours before serving.

Yield: One 9-inch (23-cm) cake, or 8 to 10 slices

Petit Fours

These lovely little treats are sure to impress any guest.

For Cake:

1½ cups (185 g) plus 2 tablespoons (15 g) all-purpose flour

1½ cups (300 g) sugar

1 teaspoon (4.6 g) baking powder

¾ teaspoon salt

¼ cup (55 g) plus 2 tablespoons (28 g) non-hydrogenated, non-dairy butter

1 cup (235 ml) water

1 tablespoon (15 ml) lemon juice

Zest of 1 whole lemon

¾ cup (175 ml) soymilk

1 teaspoon (5 ml) vanilla extract

1 teaspoon (5 ml) lemon extract

For Petit Fours:

1½ cups (265 g) vegan chocolate chips

1 tablespoon (15 ml) vanilla extract

1 teaspoon (2.2 g) groumd nutmeg

1 cake (recipe above)

½ cup store-bought marzipan

Fondant (recipe below)

Powdered sugar, for sprinkling

For Fondant:

2½ cups (500 g) sugar

½ cup (120 ml) water

¼ cup (59 ml) corn syrup

1 tablespoon (15 ml) vanilla extract

To make cake: Preheat oven to 350°F (180°C or gas mark 4).

Brush oil on a 10 x 15-inch (23 x 23-cm) jellyroll pan, then cover with two sheets parchment paper. Pull paper over edges to ease process of popping out cake.

In a large bowl, combine flour, sugar, baking powder, and salt. Add butter, water, and lemon juice and beat well. Add remaining ingredients and continue to beat until smooth.

Pour batter into prepared pan and bake for 25 to 30 minutes, or until golden brown. Let cool completely.

Once cool, lift entire cake from pan and lay on a large cutting surface. With a serrated knife, carefully cut into two identical halves. Set aside.

To make petit fours: In a small bowl, melt chocolate chips. Add vanilla and nutmeg and continue stirring until chocolate melts completely and is warm. Gently spread sauce onto one cake half. Place other half on top, forming a sandwich.

Next, divide marzipan in half. Knead until soft, then roll out each half separately. Roll pieces until each will cover half the cake. Brush one side with dab of water, then place on top of cake, water-side down. Trim edges. Repeat with second marzipan piece. Cover and refrigerate overnight.

The next day, cut cake into 1½-inch (4-cm) cubes. Cover, then place back in refrigerator.

To make fondant: Heat sugar, water, and corn syrup to "soft ball" stage on a candy thermometer (237°F [114°C]). Pour liquid into food processor and add vanilla. Blend for 2 to 3 minutes, or until syrup becomes opaque.

Place petit fours on cooling rack and pour fondant into a small bowl. (Microwave for a few seconds if fondant has cooled.) Dip each petit four carefully into fondant, using a spoon to ice top. Sprinkle with powdered sugar once cooled.

Yield: 30 petit fours

Lady Fingers

These little treats are great when sprinkled with powdered sugar or dipped into a steaming mug of hot chocolate.

2 cups (250 g) all-purpose flour	1 teaspoon (2.7 g) cornstarch
1 cup (200 g) sugar	1 teaspoon (5 ml) vanilla extract
1 tablespoon (14 g) baking powder	¼ cup (59 ml) canola oil
	1⅔ cups (390 ml) water

Preheat oven to 375°F (190°C or gas mark 5).

In a large bowl, combine all ingredients and mix until smooth. Pour batter into greased 9 x 13-inch (23 x 33-cm) pan and bake for 40 minutes.

Let cool, then slice into strips. Turn up oven to 400°F (200°C or gas mark 6). Place strips on clean, ungreased cookie sheet and bake for another 15 to 18 minutes.

Yield: 4½ dozen lady fingers

Tasty Tidbit

- Also called *boudoir biscuits*, Lady Fingers are a light, spongy cake.

Sunday Cinnamon Rolls

These cinnamon rolls are perfect for munching on a lazy weekend morning, alongside a hot cup of tea (or a teeny scoop of vanilla ice cream!). Add 1 cup (145 g) of raisins to the dough for fruit bursts in every bite!

For Rolls:

1 cup (235 ml) soymilk

1 cup (220 g) non-hydrogenated, non-dairy butter, divided

1 cup (235 ml) water

1 tablespoon (12 g) active dry yeast

1 cup (200 g) sugar

1 teaspoon (6 g) salt

½ banana, finely mashed

6 cups (750 g) all-purpose flour, divided

2 teaspoons (4.6 g) ground cinnamon

2 cups (300 g) dark brown sugar

For Icing:

4 cups (480 g) confectioners' sugar

2 teaspoons (10 ml) vanilla extract

¾ cup (175 ml) soymilk

¼ cup (55 g) non-hydrogenated, non-dairy butter

To make rolls: In a small saucepan, heat soymilk over low heat until bubbling, then remove and let cool. Mix in ½ cup (110 g) butter, stirring until melted. Add water, then let cool until lukewarm.

In a large bowl, combine milk mixture, yeast, sugar, salt, banana, and 2 cups (250 g) flour. Stir in remaining flour, ½ cup (60 g) at a time, beating well. When dough has pulled together, place onto floured surface and knead until elastic, 8 minutes.

In a small bowl, combine cinnamon and brown sugar and set aside.

Preheat oven to 375°F (190°C or gas mark 5).

Dividing dough in half, roll each piece into a 12 x 9-inch (30 x 23-cm) rectangle. Spread ¼ cup (55 g) butter and half of cinnamon-sugar mixture over each piece. Roll up dough, using water to seal seam.

Cut each roll into 12 slices and place onto two 9 x 13-in (23 x 33-cm) greased baking pans. Cover and let rise until almost doubled in size, approximately 1 hour.

Bake for 20 to 25 minutes, or until golden brown.

To make the icing: Combine all icing ingredients in a medium-size bowl, stirring well. Heat for 20 to 25 seconds in a microwave, then drizzle over warm rolls.

Yield: 24 rolls

Eggs: Who Needs 'Em?

In vegan baking, the challenge of cooking without eggs can prove quite arduous, especially when a recipe calls for a large amount of them. Fortunately, with a little knowledge—and practice—it's easy to overcome this obstacle.

Just as there are meat substitutes such as tofu, tempeh, and seitan, there are also substitutes for eggs. For one, the commercial Ener-G Egg Replacer is a reliable alternative available in most grocery and health food stores.

But there are other, more creative ways to replace eggs in recipes. Here's a list of natural food combinations that provide the same texture, leavening, and binding functions as 1 egg:

- ¼ cup (56 g) plain soft tofu, puréed

- ½ banana, mashed

- ¼ cup (60 g) applesauce

- ¼ cup (56 g) mashed potatoes

- ¼ cup (61 g) canned pumpkin or squash

- 1¼ cup (44 g) puréed prunes

- 1 tablespoon (8 g) ground flaxseed + 3 tablespoons (45 ml) water

- 2 tablespoons (16 g) potato starch

- 2 tablespoons (28 ml) water + 1 tablespoon (15 ml) vegetable oil + 2 tablespoons (28 g) baking powder

If you need a replacement for 1 egg white, try 1 tablespoon (14 g) plain agar powder dissolved in 1 tablespoon (15 ml) water, whipped, chilled, whipped, chilled, and whipped again.

Keep in mind that some substitutes will work better in certain recipes than others. For example, in a recipe that calls for a significant number of eggs, such as cream puffs or éclairs, puréed soft tofu will prove a more effective substitute than pumpkin or squash. Along the same lines, be aware that using bananas or applesauce as binders will add a hint of those flavors to the dessert, so plan accordingly.

Replacing eggs in non-vegan recipes can be tricky, so don't get discouraged if the adapted recipe doesn't quite turn out as expected. With practice comes success and in the end, it's well worth the trouble to exclude the eggs.

Belgian Waffles

Belgian waffles are rarely eaten without accoutrements. Keep the tradition alive by topping yours with ice cream, hot fudge, and even some whipped soy topping.

2 cups (250 g) all-purpose flour

4 teaspoons (18 g) baking powder

¼ teaspoon salt

2 cups (470 ml) soymilk

¼ cup (59 ml) vegetable oil

½ ripe banana, mashed

1 teaspoon (5 ml) vanilla extract

In a large mixing bowl, combine flour, baking powder, and salt and set aside.

In a food processor, blend soymilk, vegetable oil, banana, and vanilla extract until smooth. Pour mixture into dry ingredients and stir until moistened.

Cook according to waffle iron instructions.

Yield: 10 waffles

Green Fact

The typical, omnivorous diet requires 400 gallons (1514 L) of oil each year. Cut back on oil consumption by reducing your intake of meat and dairy.

Lemon Poppy Seed Scones

"Scones" are small, biscuit-like pastries that come in various shapes and flavors. Our ingredients of choice? Lemon and poppy seeds, which, together, produce scones with a citrusy, nutty taste.

3 tablespoons (42 g) baking powder, divided

1 tablespoon (15 ml) vegetable oil

2 tablespoons (28 ml) water

2 tablespoons (28 ml) lemon juice

3 cups (375 g) all-purpose flour

1 cup (200 g) plus 1 tablespoon (12.5 g) sugar, divided

3 tablespoons (24 g) poppy seeds

2 teaspoons (4 g) grated lemon zest

1 teaspoon (6 g) salt

½ cup (110 g) plus 2 tablespoons (28 g) non-hydrogenated, non-dairy butter, cut into pieces

¼ cup (60 ml) soy creamer

¼ cup (60 ml) soymilk

Preheat oven to 375°F (190°C or gas mark 5).

In a small bowl, combine 2 tablespoons (28 g) baking powder, oil, water, and lemon juice. Mix and set aside.

In a food processor, blend flour, 1 cup (200 g) sugar, poppy seeds, remaining 1 tablespoon (14 g) baking powder, lemon zest, and salt. Add butter and blend until mixture resembles coarse meal.

Add mixture from small bowl and process until moist clumps form. Mix in soy creamer and soymilk and process until dough comes together, adding more milk if necessary.

Using floured hands, gather dough into a ball and flatten into an 8-inch (20-cm) round. Cut into 8 triangular wedges.

Transfer pieces to large baking sheet and brush with soymilk. Sprinkle with remaining 1 tablespoon (12.5 g) sugar.

Bake for 25 minutes or until scones are golden brown. Transfer to a rack and cool.

Yield: 8 scones

Banana Chocolate Mousse

*Raw foods are good for the human body and spirit. Just look at this Banana Chocolate Mousse (**pictured at right**). It provides rich nutrients and flavor, making it great after any meal.*

¼ cup (45 g) pitted Medjool dates

¼ cup (60 ml) real maple syrup

½ teaspoon vanilla extract

2 to 3 bananas, mashed

¼ cup (20 g) cocoa powder

¼ cup (60 ml) water

Soak dates in warm water for 15 to 20 minutes to soften. Drain, then combine dates, maple syrup, and vanilla in a food processor and blend until smooth.

Add bananas and cocoa powder, and blend. Add water and continue to blend until smooth. Serve immediately.

Store in a sealed, air-tight container in the refrigerator for up to 3 days or in the freezer for up to 2 weeks.

Yield: 2 cups (475 ml)

Chocolate Amaretto Fudge

It's very difficult to find great vegan fudge. Try this homemade recipe for rich, smooth chocolate with a fantastic amaretto swirl.

3 tablespoons (42 g) non-hydrogenat-ed, non-dairy butter, divided, plus more for greasing

2 ¾ cups (550 g) sugar

4 ounces (110 g) unsweetened vegan chocolate

1 cup (235 ml) soy creamer

1 tablespoon (15 ml) corn syrup

1 tablespoon (15 ml) vanilla extract

¾ cup (175 ml) amaretto liqueur

Grease an 8 x 8-inch (20 x 20-cm) pan with butter and set aside.

In a heavy-bottomed saucepan, combine sugar, chocolate, 1 ½ tablespoons (21 g) butter, soy creamer, and corn syrup. Over medium heat, stir until sugar dissolves and chocolate melts.

Bring to a boil, then reduce heat to medium low, cover, and boil for 3 minutes or until mixture reaches 234° F (112° C) on a candy thermometer.

Remove from heat and add remaining 1 ½ tablespoons (21 g) butter. Do not stir. Let mixture cool, then add vanilla and amaretto and blend. Pour into prepared pan and let sit until firm. Store in an airtight container for up to 1 week.

Yield: Sixty-four 1-inch (2.5-cm) pieces

Acknowledgments

Truly an international effort between family, friends, and supporters, this book is dedicated to those who contributed to making this project a reality. I would like to thank the following people for their enthusiasm, dedication, and continuous support: Damion Lord, Nora Meiners, James Turner, Richard Murphy, Mr. "Baby" West, Barbara Lee and Charlie, Jimmy Walker, William Grant, Bruno Caesar, Alex (Abdul) Kettles, and Stuart Patterson.

Our publisher, Will Kiester, editors Amanda Waddell and Michele Wilson, creative director Rosalind Wanke, and art director Sylvia McArdle, as well as our photographers Jack Richmond and Eric Michael, and food stylist Catrine Kelty. This project would not have been possible if not for your continual patience, hard work, and creativity.

Marc L. Cooper, Jennifer Vickery, and our photo guy Eric Pearson, thank you.

The official taste-testing team in our Boston-based igloo: Lindsay Tomlinson, Lauren Correia, Becca Carey, Amy Suguitan, Paige Clark, Cady Vishniac, Julie Walz, and Michelle Kanehe; as well as the official Black Label taste-testing team, Ashley Bear, Emily Shannon, and Lady Dominique Skye.

I would additionally like to thank Max, for bringing me to Paris, and her grand-mother Estee, for teaching me the ropes. Estee, you are a superstar! I continue to follow your words of wisdom every day, pushing the boundaries of taste and flavor.

To all my European people, who supported me when I didn't have a shop, or fancy packaging, or a marketing plan. From the streets of Paris to the nightclubs of Ibiza, we rocked with nothing but talent.

Finally, we couldn't have looked so good for so many years without the skills of two incredible designers in London, who have always created animal-friendly fashions for us: Ozwald Boateng and John Lobb. Please help us keep looking smart and sexy.

About the "Inside Scoop"

Wheeler del Torro learned to create his delicious, healthy vegan ice cream in Paris, inspired by the great Parisian Berthillon ice cream shop. The founder and owner of Wheeler's Frozen Dessert Company, a microcreamery in Boston, Wheeler crafts vegan ice cream using soy, coconut, rice, and almond milks. His ice cream has been featured in *Boston Magazine* and on the popular website Daily Candy.

General Index

A

açai berries, 19, 93
adzuki beans. *See* red beans.
agave nectar, 87, 97, 139
almond milk, 18
almonds, 26, 55, 56, 58, 120, 131
amaretto liqueur, 232
amino acids, 100
animal agriculture, 72, 77, 81, 141, 151, 157, 180, 192, 206, 216, 230
animal-feeding operations (AFOs), 72
anise extract, 28, 177
antioxidant boost, 93, 96
apple cider, 160
apples, 19, 77, 152, 154, 156, 186, 194
apricots, 19, 76, 87, 98
armagnac, 162
aromatherapy, 89
arrowroot, 16–17
avocados, 19, 91, 147

B

bananas, 19, 63, 116, 169, 232, 233
bars, 210, 212. *See also* cookies.
basil, 28, 68, 92, 191
beans. *See* specific kinds of beans.
beer, 139, 141
beeswax, 215
berries, 62, 73, 76, 93, 96, 100, 116, 138, 161, 197, 206. *See also* specific kinds of berries.
biscotti, 140, 213
blackberries, 19, 74, 75, 90, 96
black currants, 20, 124
black raspberries, 20, 46, 47
black sesame seeds, 26, 109
blackstrap molasses, 50, 169
blondies, 212
blueberries, 20, 62, 194
Boston cream pie, 219
bourbon, 162
brain power, 91
Brazilian pink pepper, 28
Brazil nuts, 26, 188
brownies, 210, 212

brown sugar, 167, 202
butternut squash, 20
buying locally, 65, 67, 102

C

cakes, 150
    cream cake, 224
    cupcakes, 222
    ice cream cakes, 225
    lady fingers, 227
    madeleines, 220
    petit fours, 226–227
    Twinkies, 221
calcium, 57
cancer, 69, 136
cantaloupe, 20, 70
cappuccino, 166
capsaicin, 86
caramel, 48, 49, 167, 186, 205
carcinogens, 69
cardamom, 28, 89, 180
carobs, 26, 98, 99
carrots, 20, 173
Carya, 55
cashew apple, 113. *See also* cashew fruit.
cashew fruit, 20, 113
cashew milk, 18
cashews, 146
cayenne pepper, 28
champagne, 197
cherries, 20, 45, 112, 130, 151
chestnuts, 26, 145
chile peppers, 22, 86, 114, 172, 192. *See also* jalapeño peppers.
chocolate, 37, 42, 51, 53, 63, 103, 122, 148, 164, 197, 218, 219, 222, 225, 232. *See also* chocolate chips; cocoa powder.
chocolate chip cookies, 214
chocolate chips, 37, 38, 42, 51, 93, 103, 114, 140, 146, 148, 197, 200, 210, 212, 213, 214, 218, 219, 222, 225, 226–227
chocolate mousse, 232, 233
cinnamon, 28, 90, 147, 228
cinnamon rolls, 228

classic flavors, 35–59
cleansing, 84
cocoa beans, 37
cocoa powder, 26, 37, 38, 39, 40, 41, 78, 114, 140, 146, 148, 150, 166, 202, 210, 214, 222, 225, 232
coconut, 20, 130, 193
coconut extract, 97, 130
coconut milk, 18, 130, 193
coffee, 58, 59, 140, 164, 166, 167. *See also* cappuccino; espresso; espresso beans.
compotes, 45, 204
cones, 139, 200
    Chocolate-Dipped Sugar Cones, 200
    Waffle Cones, 139
confectioners' glaze, 215
confits, 90, 204
consommés, 74, 204
cookies, 42, 120, 131
    biscotti, 140, 213
    chocolate chip cookies, 214
    madeleines, 220
    mini sandwich cookies, 218
    oatmeal cookies, 189, 216
    sugar cookies, 215
    wafers, 131
coulis, 73, 204
counter-top ice cream makers, 32
cranberries, 21
Crohn's disease, 109
cucumbers, 21, 108, 171
cupcakes, 222, 223
currants, 20, 124
curry, 97, 114

D

dairy products, 109, 229, 230
dandelions, 28, 100
danishes, 154
dark chocolate, 53, 93
dates, 21, 81, 232
desserts, 209–233
dragon fruit, 21, 102
Dreyer, William, 41

E

Earl Grey tea, 163
eggs, substitutions for, 229
Einstein, Albert, 220
electric ice cream makers, 31–32
energy boost, 87
environment, the, 65, 67, 72, 157, 160, 163, 187, 212, 230
espresso, 167.
    See also espresso beans.
espresso beans, 164, 165
essential oils, 97
eucalyptus extract, 29, 125

F

factory farms, 151, 192. *See also* animal agriculture.
fiber boost, 98
figs, 21, 64, 65, 97, 101, 114, 128
flavor extracts, 33
flaxseed, 26, 94
flowers, 28–30, 100
foams, 204
focus, 90
fondants, 164, 204, 226–227
food-prep methods, 204
fruits, 19–25, 61–81, 108, 111, 113. *See also* specific fruits.
    buying locally, 65, 67
fruit salad, 113
fudge, 232. *See* hot fudge.

G

gelatin, 40
ginger, 29, 89, 121, 131, 222, 223
ginger beer, 139, 141
ginkgo, 29, 90
Ginkgo biloba, 90
ginkgo nuts, 90
ginseng, 29, 89, 176
global warming, 160
goji berries, 21, 116
graham crackers, 148, 150
grains, 180
granola, 168
grapefruit, 22, 69, 91
grapes, 22
green tea, 122, 123
guava, 22, 128, 129

H

hazelnuts, 27, 87, 106
healing power, 103

heart health, 91, 136, 173
herbs, 28–30. *See also* specific herbs.
honeydew melon, 22, 70, 71
hot fudge, 202, 203
hot peppers. *See* chile peppers.

I

ice cream cakes, 150, 225
ice cream makers, 31–33
ice cream sandwiches, 148, 193, 218
ice cream tasting parties, hosting, 158–159
immune boost, 102
ingredients, 16–30

J

jackfruit, 22, 181
Jackson, James C., 168
jalapeño peppers, 22, 172.
    See also chile peppers.
jasmine extract, 29, 177
jelly, 171

K

key limes, 22, 138

L

lady fingers, 227
lavender, 29, 84, 85, 182, 183
legumes, 26–27, 180
lemonade, 161
lemongrass, 29, 193
lemon juice, 231
lemons, 22, 91. *See also* lemon juice; lemon zest.
lemon zest, 222
licorice root, 30, 184, 185
limes, 22, 138, 187, 191.
    See also key limes.
locally grown food, 102
lychees, 23, 131

M

madeleines, 220
magnesium boost, 101
mangoes, 23, 124
manual ice cream makers, 31
maple syrup, 55
marshmallows, 40, 148
marzipan, 226–227
meat, 230. *See also* animal agriculture.

melba sauce, 125
melons. *See* specific kinds of melon.
memory, 90
metabolism boost, 86
Mexican chocolate, 53, 103
milks, 18, 57. *See also* specific milks.
milkshakes, 176
mini sandwich cookies, 218
mint, 39, 84, 187
molasses, 50, 169
Moore, George Edward, 127
mousse, 232

N

nectarines, 23, 66
non-dairy milks, 18. *See also* specific milks.
nutmeg, 30, 186
nuts, 26–27, 146. *See also* specific kinds of nuts.

O

oatmeal cookies, 189, 216
oats, 27, 96, 101, 189, 216, 217
oranges, 23, 68, 102, 134, 135

P

pancakes, 121
papaya, 23, 74, 75
parsley, 23
passion fruit, 24, 135
pastries
    cinnamon rolls, 228
    danishes, 154
    scones, 231
peaches, 24, 155, 178
peanut butter, 51, 94, 95, 169, 170, 171, 193, 205, 210
peanuts, 27
pears, 24, 56, 80, 194
pecans, 27, 53, 54, 55, 146, 154
peppercorns, 28, 181
peppermint, 30, 39, 84, 187
peppers. *See* chile peppers.
pesticides, 187
petit fours, 226–227
pies, 219
pineapple, 24, 45, 68, 130, 132, 135
pine nuts, 27
pink peppercorns, 28, 181
pistachio nuts, 27, 57, 136, 140
plums, 24, 49, 67
pollution, 72

pomegranates, 24, 72, 91
poppy seeds, 231
Port reductions, 204
potassium boost, 101
pretzels, 146
protein, 173
protein power, 94
prune juice, 162
pudding, 117
pumpkin, 24, 144, 189
pumpkin seeds, 78
purées, 56, 128

R

rainforests, 212
raisins, 162, 216
raspberries, 20, 24, 46, 47, 66,
    100, 122, 125, 138, 172
ratatouilles, 132, 133, 204
red beans, 27, 117
refreezing, 33
restoration, 89
rhubarb, 25, 73
riboflavin, 119
rice milk, 18
rolls, 228
rosemary, 30, 97, 184
rose water, 30, 178, 179, 180
rum, 141

S

saffron, 30, 155
salads, 161
salsa, 124, 168
sandwich cookies, 218
sandwiches, 193, 218
sauces, 199–207. See also toppings.
scones, 231
seaweed, 118, 119
seeds, 26–27. See also specific
    kinds of seeds.
self-freezing ice cream makers, 32
semisweet dark chocolate, 53
serving suggestions. See sides;
    toppings.
sesame seeds, 26, 109
shandys, 139
sides, 209–233. See also toppings.
    biscotti, 213
    blondies, 212, 213
    Boston cream pie, 219
    brownies, 210
    cakes, 220, 222, 224, 227

cookies, 131, 213, 214, 215,
    216, 218
cupcakes, 222
lady fingers, 227
madeleines, 220
petit fours, 226–227
pies, 219
sandwich cookies, 218
Twinkies, 221
s'mores, 148, 149
sorbets, 78, 79, 139, 141, 162,
    194, 196, 197
soy creamer, 16
soymilk, 16, 18, 54
spices, 28–30, 103, 113, 124,
    168
sponge cake, 80
star fruit, 25, 132
strawberries, 25, 46, 138, 161, 197
stress relief, 92
sugar, 17, 167
sugar cones, 200, 201
sugar cookies, 215
"sushi," 111
sweet potatoes, 92, 106, 156
syrups, 66

T

tarragon, 30, 181
tartare, 76
tasting parties, 158–159
tea, 122, 163
tempura, 108
Thai chile peppers, 114, 192
toffee, 50
toppings, 199–207. See also
    fruits; sides.
    berry sauce, 206
    butterscotch, 202
    caramel sauce, 205
    chocolate-covered fruit, 122, 197
    compotes, 45, 204
    confits, 90, 204
    consommés, 74, 204
    coulis, 73, 204
    crumbles, 144
    foams, 204
    fondants, 164, 204
    fruits, 97, 122, 155, 156, 197
    hot fudge, 202
    jackfruit sauce, 181
    melba sauce, 125

nuts, 106
peanut butter sauce, 94, 95, 205
Port reductions, 204
purées, 128
ratatouilles, 132, 204
salsa, 124, 168
syrups, 66
tartare, 76
tempura, 108
Twinkies, 221

V

vanilla extract, 17, 36, 86, 87, 88,
    89, 150, 155, 188, 222,
    226–227
vegan ice cream
    nutritional content of, 14
veganism, 9–11, 13, 86. See also
    vegetarianism.
    benefits to the environment, 81
    environmental benefits of, 160,
        163, 187, 230
    health benefits of, 98, 188
vegetables, 19–25. See also
    specific vegetables.
    buying locally, 65, 67
vegetarianism, 13, 141. See also
    veganism.
    environmental benefits of, 230
    health benefits of, 98, 188
vessels, 199–207
vitamin A, 100
vitamin B12, 40
vitamin B2, 119. See also riboflavin.

W

wafers, 131
waffles, 230
Wakefield, Ruth, 42, 214
walnuts, 27, 55, 210
wasabi, 30, 110, 111
water chestnuts, 25
watermelons, 25, 132, 133
whiskey, 157

Y

yams, 25, 106, 107

Complete Recipe Index

A

Almond, 56
Almond Biscotti, 58
Almond Cookie, 120
Anise, 177
Aphrodisiacal Flavors, 175–197
Apple Cider, 160
Apple Martini Sorbet, 194
Apple Pie, 152, 153
Apricot, 76
Asian Flavors, 105–125
Avocado, 147
Avocado Lemon, 91

B

Banana, 63
Banana Chocolate Mousse, 232, 233
Banana Molasses, 169
Belgian Waffles, 230
Berries Galore, 62
Black Currant Tea, 124
Black Raspberry, 46, 47
Black Sesame, 109
Blackberry and Oats, 96
Blackberry Confit, 90
Blackberry Consommé, 74, 75
Blondies, 212
Blueberry, 62
Blueberry Martini Sorbet, 194
Bon Bons, 183
Boston Cream Pie, 219
Bourbon Raisin, 162
Brown Sugar Caramel, 167
Bubble Gum, 44
Butter Pecan, 52, 53
Butter Toffee, 50
Butterscotch, 49, 202

C

Cantaloupe, 70
Cappuccino, 166
Caramel, 48
Caramel Sauce, 205
Caramelized Apples, 186
Cardamom Rose, 180
Caribbean and Island Flavors, 127–141

Caribbean Coffee, 140
Carob Apricot, 98, 99
Carrot Cake, 173
Cashew Fruit, 113
Champagne Sorbet, 196, 197
Cherries Jubilee, 45
Cherry Blossom, 112
Cherry Pie, 151
Chestnut, 145
Chocolate, 37
Chocolate Amaretto Fudge, 232
Chocolate Chip Biscotti, 213
Chocolate Chip Brownies with Chocolate Icing, 210
Chocolate Chip Cookie Dough, 42, 43
Chocolate Chip Cookies, 214
Chocolate Chip Ice Cream Cake, 225
Chocolate Chocolate Chip, 38
Chocolate Chocolate Chip Cookies, 214
Chocolate-Covered Raspberries, 122
Chocolate-Covered Strawberries, 197
Chocolate Cupcakes, 222
Chocolate Cups, 53
Chocolate-Dipped Sugar Cones, 200
Chocolate Fudge Brownies, 210, 211
Chocolate Icing, 210
Chocolate Marshmallow, 40
Chocolate Martini Sorbet, 194, 195
Chocolate Mint-Chocolate Chip, 39
Chocolate Peanut Butter Swirl, 51
Chocolate Pretzel, 146
Chocolate Pretzel Nut, 146
Cinnamon Basil, 191
Cinnamon Ginkgo, 90
Cinnamon Juniper, 147
Coconut, 130
Coconut Cherry, 130
Coconut Lemongrass, 193
Coconut Pineapple, 130
Coffee, 58

Cookies 'N Cream, 42
Crispy Caramelized Hazelnuts, 106
Crispy Ginger Almond Wafer, 131
Crunch Chocolate Balls, 63
Crunchy Peanut Butter Sauce, 94, 95
Cupcakes, 222, 223

D

Dark-and-Stormy Sorbet, 141
Dark Chocolate Açai Berry, 93
Date, 81

E

Earl Grey, 163
Espresso, 167
Espresso Bean, 164, 165
Eucalyptus, 125

F

Fig, 64, 65
Fig Purée, 128
French Madeleines, 220
Fresh Balsamic Berries Tartare, 76
Fresh Berry Coulis, 73
Fresh Mint Lime, 187
Fried Asian Pancakes, 121
Fruit "Sushi," 111
Fruit Tempura, 108
Fruity Flavors, 61–81

G

Gin-Infused Peaches, 178
Ginger Beer Sorbet, 141
Ginger Cupcakes, 222, 223
Ginger Ginseng, 89
Ginger Lychee, 131
Ginseng, 176
Goji Berry Banana, 116
Granola Crunch, 168
Grapefruit, 69
Green Apple, 77
Green Tea, 122, 123
Grilled Figs with Rosemary and Agave, 97
Grilled Plums, 49
Guava, 128, 129

...rs, 83–103
...w, 70, 71
...nocolate Fondant, 164
...ot Fudge, 202, 203

I
Ice Cream Cake, 150
Ice Cream Sides and Desserts, 209–233
Island-Green Pistachio, 136, 137
Italian White Cream Cake, 224

J
Jackfruit Sauce, 181
Jalapeño, 172
Jasmine, 177

K
Key Lime, 138

L
Lady Fingers, 227
Lavender, 182, 183
Lavender Mint, 84, 85
Lemon Basil, 191
Lemon Cupcakes, 222, 223
Lemon Poppy Seed Scones, 231
Lemonade, 161
Licorice, 184, 185
Lime Basil, 191

M
Maple Almond, 55
Maple Pecan, 55
Maple Walnut, 55
Milkshake, 176
Mini Sandwich Cookies, 218
Mint Chocolate Chip, 39
Mojito Sorbet, 194

N
Nectarine, 66
New York Irish Cream, 157
Novelty Flavors, 143–173
Nutmeg, 186

O
Oatmeal Cookie Bars, 189
Oatmeal Raisin Cookies, 216, 217
Oats and Figs, 101
Orange, 68
Orange-Basil Marinated Pineapple, 68
Orange Dragon Fruit, 102
Orange Mojito Sorbet, 194

Orange Passion Fruit, 134, 135
Orange Pineapple, 135

P
Papaya, 74, 75
Peanut Butter, 51
Peanut Butter and Jelly, 170, 171
Peanut Butter Banana, 169
Peanut Butter Brownies, 210
Peanut Butter Cucumber, 171
Peanut Butter Flaxseed, 94, 95
Peanut Butter Ice Cream Sandwiches, 193
Peanut Butter Sauce, 205
Pear, 80
Pear Martini Sorbet, 194
Pear Purée, 56
Pecan Apple Danish, 154
Petit Fours, 226–227
Pie Crust Crumbles, 144
Pink Pepper Tarragon, 181
Pistachio, 57
Pistachio Chocolate Biscotti, 140
Plum, 67
Pomegranate, 72
Pomegranate Champagne Sorbet, 197
Pomegranate Grapefruit, 91
Praline Pecan, 54
Prune Armagnac Sorbet, 162
Pumpkin, 144
Pumpkin and Oats, 189

R
Raspberry Dandelion, 100
Raspberry Jalapeño, 172
Raspberry Key Lime, 138
Raspberry Melba, 125
Raspberry Syrup, 66
Red Bean, 117
Red Bean Pudding, 117
Rhubarb, 73
Roasted Agave Apricots, 87
Roasted Peaches, 155
Roasted Pineapple Compote, 45
Rocky Road, 41
Rose Water, 178, 179
Rosemary, 184

S
Salted Chocolate Pumpkin Seeds, 78
Seaweed, 118, 119

Shandy, 139
Slow-Roasted Green Apples, 156
S'more, 148
S'more Sandwiches, 148, 149
"Spaghetti" Ice Cream with Brownie "Meatballs," 36
Spicy Cherry Salsa, 168
Spicy Chocolate Chocolate Chocolate Chip, 103
Spicy Chocolate Twist, 103
Spicy Fruit Salad, 113
Spicy Mango Salsa, 124
Sponge Cake, 80
Star Fruit, 132
Strawberry, 46
Strawberry Key Lime, 138
Strawberry Salad, 161
Sugar Cones, 200, 201
Sugar Cookies with Icing and Sprinkles, 215
Sunday Cinnamon Rolls, 228
Sweet Basil, 190, 191
Sweet Cucumber, 108
Sweet Curry Coconut, 97
Sweet Curry Fig, 114, 115
Sweet Ginger Tea, 121
Sweet Potato, 156
Sweet Potato Basil, 92

T
Thai Chile, 192
Thai Chile Chocolate, 114
Toffee, 50
Twinkies, 221

V
Vanilla, 36
Vanilla Brazil Nut, 188
Vanilla Cardamom, 88, 89
Vanilla Chile Pepper, 86
Vanilla Graham Cracker, 150
Vanilla Hazelnut, 87
Vanilla Saffron, 155
Very Berry Sauce, 206, 207

W
Waffle Cones, 139
Wasabi, 110, 111
Watermelon Pineapple Ratatouille, 132, 133
Watermelon Sorbet, 78, 79

Y
Yam, 106, 107